T0334471

Advance Praise for

Touch the Wounds

"One of the most profound meditations on suffering, from a Christian perspective, that I have ever read."
— James Martin, SJ, author of *Learning to Pray*

"Tomáš Halík's *Touch the Wounds* is a masterfully written, personal, and at the same time critical book that brings into dialogue contemporary life experience, biblical message, mystical tradition, and modern criticism of religion, all showing how in the wounds of our world as Christians we touch the wounds of God not by turning away from suffering but by confronting it. A fascinating, challenging, and encouraging vision."
— Cardinal Walter Kasper, president emeritus of the Pontifical Council for Promoting Christian Unity

"What we need now is the voice of a prophet in the tradition of Jeremiah, Ezekiel, and Isaiah, who were unafraid to confront hypocrisy in high places and fearless in identifying the self-inflicted wounds of a society in desperate need of a particular and urgent healing touch. That prophetic voice for our time and our world belongs to Tomáš Halík, an impressive scholar who writes with flawless grace and instinct so that truth is disclosed page after page in his latest, powerful book."
— Doris Donnelly, editor of *Sacraments and Justice*

"In this deeply personal narrative, Tomáš Halík invokes the figure of Thomas, less to affirm the importance of doubt in religious life than to remind us that Christian faith passes through our wounds and through the reality of pain and suffering. As ever, Halík manages to offer a fresh and hopeful Christian message without condemning the secular world."

—Catherine Cornille, co-author of *Christian Identity between Secularity and Plurality*

"Tomáš Halík's *Touch the Wounds* is an elegant and profound set of meditations on the place and purpose and meaning of suffering. Halík shows that, and how, attention to suffering is attention to Jesus, and, therefore, a means of entry for Christians into the world's healing. It is a lovely book, and an inspiring one."

—Paul J. Griffiths, author of *Regret: A Theology*

"*Touch the Wounds* will be a source of great insight and inspiration for seekers, drawn potentially to Christian faith, and will liberate many others from stultifying forms of false certainty. It will open others again to ecumenical exchanges that will enrich their faith. The world needs more Tomáš Halík."

—Charles Taylor, co-author of *Reconstructing Democracy*

"Tomáš Halík is one of the most insightful voices in contemporary Catholicism, and his book on the wounded church and sin in the church is a turning point in the effort to make sense of the ecclesial crisis that has taken shape in the last few years: from the new phase in the abuse crisis to the pandemic."

—Massimo Faggioli, author of *Catholicism and Citizenship*

Touch the Wounds

Touch *the* Wounds

ON SUFFERING, TRUST, AND TRANSFORMATION

TOMÁŠ HALÍK

Translated by
GERALD TURNER

UNIVERSITY OF NOTRE DAME PRESS

Notre Dame, Indiana

University of Notre Dame Press
Notre Dame, Indiana 46556
undpress.nd.edu

Published in the United States of America

Library of Congress Control Number: 2022947573

ISBN: 978-0-268-20489-1 (Hardback)
ISBN: 978-0-268-20491-4 (WebPDF)
ISBN: 978-0-268-20488-4 (Epub)

The disbelief of Thomas has done more for our faith than the faith of the other disciples.

—St. Gregory the Great

By his wounds we have been healed.
—Isaiah 53:5

Two prisoners whose cells adjoin communicate with each other by knocking on the wall. The wall is the thing which separates them but is also their means of communication. It is the same with us and God. Every separation is a link.

—Simone Weil

CONTENTS

The central message of this book can be summed up in a few sentences. The painful wounds of our world are Christ's wounds. If we ignore pain, poverty, and suffering in our world, if we turn a blind eye to them out of indifference or cowardice, if we are unwilling to acknowledge the injuries we inflict (including the injuries inflicted in our churches), and conceal them from others and ourselves with masks, cosmetics, or tranquilizing drugs, then we have no right to say to Christ, like Thomas the apostle when he touched Jesus's wounds: "My Lord and my God."

In the Gospels, the resurrected Jesus identifies himself with his wounds. They are the proof of his identity. The wounded Christ is the real, living Christ. He shows us his wounds and gives us the courage not to conceal our own: we are permitted our own wounds. Our faith may also be wounded by doubts. Wounded faith is more Christian, not less.

I am writing the preface to the English translation of my book at a time when the pandemic of a destructive disease is coming to a head on our planet. Every morning I have to reassure myself that I really am awake, that I haven't moved from one dream to another or wandered into some sci-fi horror movie.

We're part of a world full of wounds. For many people, the dark cloud of pain conceals the certainty of faith; the face of a benevolent God is hidden in the darkness that we are passing through together. But the Easter scene that inspired this book can speak to us with enormous urgency precisely at such a time. It is through Jesus's wounds that the apostle Thomas sees God.

Let us not seek God in the storms and earthquakes. A God enthroned somewhere beyond the world, sending upon his children cruel punishments, the like of which would rightly land any parent in court, truly does not exist, thankfully. Atheists rightly maintain that such a god is simply a projection of our fears and desires. The vengeful god used by preachers, who trade on the world's misfortunes to arouse fear and exploit it for their religious ends, is simply a product and servant of their own vindictiveness: they use it as a stick to beat people that they hate, and as a curse and punishment for what they themselves reject or fear. Their god of vengeance is simply a fictitious extension of their own malice and vindictiveness. When they brandish a God who punishes us with wars, natural disasters, and disease, they commit the sin of invoking God's name in vain. They are replacing the father of Jesus with a bloodthirsty pagan idol that thrives on the blood of human sacrifice.

Like the prophet Elijah on Mount Horeb, we are more likely to find God in a quiet breeze—in the unaffected expressions of love and solidarity, and in everyday heroism generated in the dark hours of calamities. It is in those expressions of love and service, which restore our hope and the courage to live and not give up, that true holiness manifests itself. That is where God happens.

We can observe the wounds of this world in the way that Pilate observed the scourged Jesus: *Ecce homo!* Behold the man! Is this man covered in wounds, "without dignity, without beauty," really a man still? The mob to which Pilate shows Christ, covered in wounds, is like a wild beast, incensed even more by the smell of blood: Crucify him!

But on the way to the Crucifixion Veronica emerges from the crowd. Jesus imprints the image of his face forever on the veil of compassion. Whoever wipes the sweat and blood from the wounds of our world may see and preserve the face of Christ. And whoever, like "doubting Thomas," gazes from the gloom of doubts at the wounds on the body of our world and in the hearts of our neighbors may—precisely through that wounded humanity, through that image of the humanity that the Son of God took upon himself—see God. "I and the Father are one," said the one who bore our wounds.

Scripture expresses the unity of the Father and the Son not in dogmatic definitions but in a dramatic story. That drama includes the moments of painful abandonment, as witness Jesus's cry on the cross. Sometimes the time between the darkness of the cross and the dawn of Sunday morning is long and arduous. The present book seeks also to address those who are enduring such moments—and it is not intended to offer them "religious opium," sweet-sounding clichés of cheap pious reassurance.

Let us not expect faith to provide the answers to every question. Instead we should derive from it the courage to step into the cloud of mystery and bear life's many open questions and paradoxes. St. Paul tells us that here on earth we see only in part, as in a mirror, as in a riddle. Faith mustn't stop seeking and questioning; it must not petrify into an ideology. It must not abandon its openness to an eschatological future.

As I write these lines I vividly recall the Easter of this tragic year: Easter with empty and often-locked churches, Easter without public religious services. But this Easter in particular made a profound impression on me.

For one thing it reminded me strikingly of those eleven years when I served "clandestinely" as a secretly ordained priest at the time of communist persecution. In those days I also celebrated Easter in private homes in a circle of my closest associates, at an ordinary table with no chasuble or golden chalice, no organ or incense.

And for another, I experienced it as a sort of prophetic vision of warning: unless the church (and not only our "Roman Church") does not undergo the profound reform called for by Pope Francis—not only a structural reform but above all a turning to the depths, to the very heart of the gospel—then empty and locked churches will not be the exception but rather the rule. This is already happening in many European countries, not only in countries of eastern and central Europe (such as my own country, the Czech Republic), which underwent "hard secularization" at the time of the communist regimes (and where the anticipated great religious revival after for the fall of the communist regimes hasn't happened), but also in western and now also southern Europe, where "soft secularization" is under way. Even traditionally Catholic countries like Ireland, Spain, and Italy are undergoing rapid secularization. And now it looks as if Poland, too, is in line. Likewise, the assertion of many sociologists that the weakening of traditional church religiosity is only a

European problem and does not affect North and South America turns out to be illusory. Maybe the word *secularization* is too "played out" to capture the full breadth and depth of this process, but the "wounding," weakening, and malaise of a certain type of traditional religion—however we describe the situation—cannot be denied.

The crisis of ecclesial Christianity is not due primarily to some dangerous forces from outside—"the tsunami of secularism, consumerism, and materialism," as we sometimes hear from the pulpit. For that reason also the crisis cannot be halted either by the present "retro-Catholicism," that fatuous attempt to return to a premodern world that is now gone, or by some hollow and superficial "modernization" in the sense of conformity to "the spirit of the age."

The "spirit of the age" (Zeitgeist, fashion) is certainly not the Holy Spirit; it is the *language of this world* to which Christians should not conform, as St. Paul wrote. Instead Christians should listen to the "signs of the times" and properly understand them. These are *the language of God* in historical events of which we are a part and that we help to create through our understanding. If we are not to project our own fears and desires too hastily onto the events we experience (i.e., if we are to free ourselves from the religion that Freud and many others have rightly criticized), we need to foster a culture of "spiritual discernment."

This is because it is not easy within the changes of cultural mentality that occasionally occur—as in the Renaissance, the Enlightenment, and the cultural revolutions of the 1960s and the present day—to discern what is "human, all too human," superficial, external, and ephemeral, and the "opportune moment" (*kairos*), which we must accept and fulfill as God's challenge to our faith and our life's praxis.

I believe that one of the fateful misapprehensions on the part of the church hierarchy was its reaction to the "ethics of authenticity" (to borrow a phrase from Charles Taylor) that emerged from the "second Enlightenment" of the 1960s. The "sexual revolution," which was part of the younger generation's rebellion against tradition and authority, particularly aroused fear and panic in a church represented by men living in celibacy. Instead of responding by developing a theology of love and sexuality drawing on the deep wellsprings of Christian mysticism, the church tended to regress to a religion of injunctions and proscriptions. In the church's documents, in its preaching and prescriptions, the entire sexuality agenda—particularly the attempt to discipline sexuality as strictly as possible—came to the fore to such a degree that it seemed that the *sextum* (the Sixth Commandment) had become the first—and possibly sole—commandment. Catholics started to be perceived as the ones who never stopped talking about condoms, abortion, and same-sex unions—until Pope Francis had the courage to aptly describe this shift of priorities as a "neurotic obsession" and to point out what really constitutes the heart of Christianity, which we had often forgotten: mercy, compassionate and solidary love toward all, particularly the marginalized, and toward our mother Earth.

The secular world's natural reaction to fiery sermons against the laxity of sexual morality was: Look to your own ranks! There followed a worldwide wave of revelations of long-concealed and denied crimes of sexual abuse by the clergy, particularly the abuse of children and adolescents. I think almost everyone knew or suspected in some way something of these and similar matters, but clearly few could have imagined the depth and extent of this painful wound. It also transpired that many of those who inveighed most vociferously against homosexuality were doing so to suppress their own private problems in this regard and that they often led a Jekyll and Hyde existence, or—in the words of Jesus—were like whitewashed tombs, beautiful on the outside but full of putrefaction on the inside.

When Pope Francis started to speak openly about the real cause of this situation, and when, in his encyclical *Amoris laetitia*, he sought to revise the religion of the Christian Pharisees and scribes by offering an ethic of love, mercy, and understanding for people in difficult situations and by encouraging trust in the voice of conscience, he aroused rabid hatred in the spiritual heirs of Jesus's enemies: the Pharisees and scribes of our day.

As Pope Francis pointed out, the chief root of these phenomena within the church was the abuse of power—clericalism. In his memorable opening speech at the summit of presidents of worldwide bishops' conferences in February 2019, Cardinal Tagle, one of the pope's closest colleagues, cited key sentences from this present book. He spoke about these painful phenomena as the wounds of Christ, which those who affirm the divinity of Christ must not ignore.

Two conflicting narratives have emerged: one downplays the evil of abuse in the church and shifts responsibility for it onto external influences, onto the "spirit of liberalism" that penetrated even the church in the 1960s and loosened its discipline; the other, the view of Pope Francis, states that those who have not come to terms with the church's loss of power in modern society started to exercise that power even more and misuse it within the church itself, particularly toward those who were the least, the weakest, and the most vulnerable. The first of these narratives is demonstrably untrue: the greatest number of cases of abuse occurred not in the period of the church's "liberalization" after the Second Vatican Council but precisely in the period of attempts to impose the most rigid discipline, the kind of Catholicism that the Council tried to free the church from. As Cardinal Schönborn pointed out, sexual crimes were most often committed by leading figures from the conservative "church movements" (*movimenti*); precisely the closed and elitist sectarian mentality and the unhealthy links with "spiritual teachers" that prevailed in those closed groups created a favorable climate for those forms of abuse of power, authority, and trust.

The period during which these concealed and therefore festering wounds started to come to light worldwide—the last years of Benedict XVI's pontificate and the entire pontificate of Pope Francis—is also a period of another "sign of the times": a radical awakening of awareness of women's dignity in society and the church. Just as the church lost its influence on the working class through its tardy reaction to the social problems of the industrial revolution, and just as it alienated a large proportion of educated members of society because of its inappropriate reaction to the turbulent developments in science and philosophy at the turn of the twentieth century (the unfortunate "antimodernist crusade"), so now, if it ignores these present changes in women's self-awareness, it risks losing many of the women who have traditionally been pillars of the church.

The disquiet and tension in the church caused by these phenomena have been concealed at the present time by the global pandemic. At this moment we can only speculate what kind of world awaits us when the dust dies down, when the proverbial grass starts to grow over the graves of the countless victims of the viral infection. How is humanity processing this experience that took us all unawares? What will be the church's response? The world will certainly change—will the church?

During this strange Easter, I once more opened a slim pamphlet by the Czech seventeenth-century thinker Jan Amos Komenský (Comenius), entitled *The Legacy of a Dying Mother, the Unity of the Brethren*. As the last bishop of this small, persecuted Protestant church, he wrote in exile this remarkable "theology of the death of the church." I was alerted to the work many years ago by one of my teachers of faith, Oto Mádr, for many years a prisoner of communism, in his essay "Modus moriendi ecclesiae" (How a church dies). "The death of the church" is once more a topical issue. Yes, I do believe that one form of the church, one form of Christianity, is truly dying. But isn't the core of Christianity the message of the death that must precede resurrection?

Yet resurrection is not "resuscitation," the return to a previous state. The Gospels tell us that Jesus was transformed beyond recognition by his experience of death. Not even his nearest and dearest could recognize him at first. He had to prove his identity by his wounds. In this book I confess that I am incapable of believing in a God without wounds, a church without wounds, or a faith without wounds. Our faith too is constantly wounded by what we experience—in the world and also in the church itself. But aren't its wounds—maybe more than a lot of other things—a sign of its authenticity? Can a faith that bears no stigmata, a faith that cautiously avoids the Golgothas of our time, help to heal a wounded world?

I would like to present my readers with witness to a faith that lives even when it is sometimes painful and bleeds.

Tomáš Halík, Easter 2020

The Gate of the Wounded

But Thomas (who was called the Twin), one of the twelve, was not with them when Jesus came. So the other disciples told him, "We have seen the Lord." But he said to them, "Unless I see the mark of the nails in his hands, and put my finger in the mark of the nails and my hand in his side, I will not believe."

A week later his disciples were again in the house, and Thomas was with them. Although the doors were shut, Jesus came and stood among them and said, "Peace be with you." Then he said to Thomas, "Put your finger here and see my hands. Reach out your hand and put it in my side. Do not doubt but believe." Thomas answered him, "My Lord and my God!" Jesus said to him, "Have you believed because you have seen me? Blessed are those who have not seen and yet have come to believe."

—John 20:24–29

After reading this Gospel I left the pulpit and returned to my seat. It was early morning in Madras Cathedral, gray, silent, and almost empty. India lay before me like a brightly colored carpet interwoven with a multitude of holy places. I was heading for Bodh Gaya, where Buddha had attained enlightenment; to Sarnat, where the Awakened One first addressed his disciples; to Varanasi, on the banks of the Ganges, the holiest of sites for Hindus; to Mathura, the birthplace of Krishna; but here in Madras, at the heart of Indian Christianity, where the tomb of Thomas the apostle, the patron saint of India, has been venerated since ancient times, I felt for a moment truly at home, thanks in part to the words of that deeply familiar text.

At that moment I still perceived that passage of John's Gospel as I always had and as it is generally interpreted, namely that by his appearance Jesus dispelled his skeptical apostle's lingering doubts about the truth of his resurrection, that "doubting Thomas" immediately became a believer. I did not suspect that before the day was out, this gospel text would address me afresh—differently and more profoundly—and that it would even reveal to me in a new light the greatest mystery of Christian faith: the resurrection of Jesus and his divine nature. Moreover, this new perception would gradually draw me onto a certain path of spirituality of which I yet knew nothing. It showed me "the gate for doubting Thomases," *the gate of the wounded.*

Christian faith is a constant penetration of our lives by the gospel, the courage to "enter the story," to reveal the meaning of the Bible stories afresh and more profoundly through our own life experience but also to allow the powerful images of the gospel to have an impact so that they may gradually illuminate, interpret, and transform the flow of our own lives.

Events, experiences, ideas, and sudden insights very often need time to mature within us and bring forth fruit. Twelve years have passed since my Indian pilgrimage. I sit here once again in the silence and solitude of my summer hermitage in the Rhineland. After last night's storm the hilltops are shrouded in a thick mist that the first rays of morning are only just beginning to slowly penetrate. All around, the valley is covered in low-lying clouds. So it is within a cloud that I start to write this book, another attempt to have my answer ready for people who ask me the reason for "the hope that I have."[1]

"God is dead. . . . *We have killed him*—you and I." I have previously quoted this fateful verdict of Nietzsche's from his book *The Gay Science*, in which the Madman (the only one who is permitted to state unpleasant truths with impunity) announces his diagnosis of the world to those who do not believe in God. He tells the world that it has lost the very foundations of its previous metaphysical and moral certainties.[2] On the other hand, one can find in another of Nietzsche's books a less familiar and less quoted passage, namely, where the death of the old deities is described: when the god of the Jews declared himself to be the only God, all the other deities are said to have burst into such derisive laughter that they laughed themselves to death.[3]

"Religion is on its way back" is the chorus from every corner of the globe. Opinions differ only about whether it is a good thing or a bad thing—and also, perhaps, about who or what is coming back, and from where. Is it the One God that is returning, "the God of Abraham, Isaac, Jacob, and Jesus" that Jews, Christians, and Muslims all believe in, or the "god of the philosophers," the Supreme Being—invented by the Enlightenment—who adorns political proclamations and the preambles to various constitutions? Is it the God who quietly responds to thirsting human hearts and heals their wounds, or the God of war and vengeance that hands out wounds? Or are we to look forward to the return of the old sniggering sarcastic deities?

It is said of St. Martin that Satan himself appeared to him in the guise of Christ. The saint was not deceived, however. "Where are your wounds?" he asked.

My spiritual openness does not mean that I espouse an ingratiating "boundless tolerance," which is more an expression of indifference and spiritual indolence if it shirks the task of carefully "distinguishing spirits." It is, after all, naive and dangerous to ignore the fact that there are destructive "images of God" and that even in the worthiest of traditions there slumber symbols, statements, and stories that can be beaten into weapons instead of plowshares. However, like everything in life that has grandeur and substance, religions comprise pitfalls and dangers. And so, with the apostle Thomas and St. Martin, I demand of all those who seek to occupy the throne vacated by the collapse of the sardonic deities, "Show me first your wounds!" For I do not believe in "faiths without wounds."

It is true that for years now I have endeavored, with respect and willingness, to study a multitude of religious paths. I've traveled a good part of the globe, and nothing of what I've seen and come to know permits me to confine myself to the logic of "either/or" (if two people say two different things, at least one of them must be wrong). I know that if someone thinks or says something different from me it may simply be because they look at things from a different standpoint, from another angle, because their traditions and experience are different, because they express themselves in a different "language"—in other words, that the difference between their viewpoint and statements and mine need not in any way deny either my or their right to the truth, or call into question their or my sincerity or integrity. I also know that this awareness need not lead to cozily complaisant relativism ("Everyone is right in their own way"); rather, it can lead to an endeavor to share the experience of one's own naturally limited horizon and broaden it through mutual dialogue in which we get to know others and ourselves better.

I have learned to respect the many different paths that people take to attain life's final mystery. I believe that the "ultimate mystery" infinitely surpasses all the notions and names that we people associate with it. Yes, I believe in one God, the Father of *all* people, and I believe that no person or "religious institution" or their professionals has a "monopoly" on God. I am confident that God is the final estuary of even the most meandering of rivers: irrespective of frontiers, different religious systems, and different cultures, the paths of all those who revere the ultimate mystery of life and who seek honestly, by the light of their traditions, their yearning for truth, their conscience, and their knowledge, will eventually lead toward God.

I am neither All-knowing nor All-seeing, and so I cannot pronounce final and infallible judgments about others and their personal beliefs because I cannot see into their hearts or catch a glimpse of the final end and goal of their journey. No one can rid me of the hope that "the God of the others" is, in the final analysis "my God," because the God I believe in is also the God of those who do not know the name by which I call God.

But in the same breath I add and declare: for me there is no other path or other gate to God than that which is opened by a wounded hand and pierced heart. I am unable to exclaim, "*My* Lord and *my* God" until I see the wound that pierced the heart. If *credere* is derived from "*cor dare*" (giving one's heart), then my heart and my faith belong only to the God that has wounds to show.

My faith is at one with my love, and no one can rid me of my love for the Crucified, which is my response to his love for me: *Can anything cut me off from the love of Christ?*[4] Can anything cut me off from that love whose proof of identity is its wounds?[5] I am incapable of uttering the words "my God" unless I see the wounds! However radiant a religious vision might be, if it lacks the "scars left by the nails" I would be hard pressed, in spite of my goodwill, to rid myself of my misgivings that it might be an illusion, or a projection of my own desires, or even the Antichrist. My God is a wounded God.

Should anyone sense in what I have just declared certain contradictions, I must add that I am equally aware of them: it is a real tension of my faith. I relate in hope and trust to a God who generously accepts the diversity of his children and whose arms are open so wide that we find it hard to understand. But that does not mean that I also cannot be "certain" where the limits of that embrace are, and I cannot naively assume that it enfolds quite simply "everything." I must maintain my respect for others and for the honesty and sincerity of their *act* of faith, but if I am to "put my heart" into something, I have to ask after its fruits.[6] In religion, just as in all other important areas of life, there are values that are fundamental and of irreplaceable worth, and there are others that only feign to be such—and they include weeds and poisonous plants. And it is not the case, as many used to think and maybe still do, that there are fields here (our own) that yield only good harvests, and others about which we can say in advance that nothing good will grow in them. The Bible both exhorts us to test "the spirits" that are proffered us[7] and warns that it is extremely hard to tell the "the darnel" from "the wheat"—indeed, that it is essentially a task impossible for us to fulfill in this world and beyond our powers of judgment.[8]

So what can I do? Make *my* faith and everything that I am required to believe undergo "St. Martin's test." I don't believe in gods and faiths that skip through the world unaffected by its pain and suffering—without scars, stripes, or burns—in order to make a smooth-tongued presentation of their glittering charms—and nothing else—in today's religious marketplace.

The point is that my faith is able to shake off the burden of doubts and feel inner certainty and the peace of home only if it climbs the steep "path of the cross," when it has its sights set on God through the narrow gate of Christ's wounds—the gate of the poor and the wounded, through which the rich, the sated, and the self-confident, the knowing and "sighted," "the healthy," "the just," "the wise and cautious" will not pass, just as the camel will not pass through the eye of the needle.[9]

Was the apostle Thomas truly freed from his doubts once and for all when he set eyes on the resurrected Christ—or had Jesus instead shown him through his wounds the one and only place where seekers and doubters can truly touch God? That was the thought that came to me that day in Madras.

On the hot afternoon of that day, my Indian colleague, a Catholic priest and professor of religious studies at the University of Madras, took me first to the place where, according to legend, the apostle Thomas was martyred, and then to a Catholic orphanage close by.[10]

During my travels to Asia, Africa, and South America, both before and since, I had looked poverty in the face, and I am familiar with moral wretchedness from my clinical practice and my experience as a confessor—the hidden torments of people's hearts and the dark recesses of human destinies. I have visited the "Golgothas of our times," the sites of Nazi and communist concentration camps, as well as Hiroshima and Ground Zero in Manhattan, places that powerfully emanate the still-vivid memories of the criminal violence perpetrated there—but even after all that, I will never forget that orphanage in Madras.

In cots that were more like poultry pens lay small, abandoned children, their stomachs swollen with hunger, tiny skeletons covered in black, often inflamed, skin. In the seemingly endless corridors their feverish eyes stared out at me from everywhere, and they stretched their pink-palmed hands out to me. In the unbreathable air, with all that stench and weeping, I felt a mental, physical, and moral nausea. I had the suffocating sense of helplessness and bitter shame that one feels when confronted with the poor and wretched, shame at having healthy skin, a full stomach, and a roof over my head. I wanted cowardly to run away as fast I could from there (and not just from there), to close my eyes and heart and forget; I recalled once more the words of Ivan Karamazov, who wanted to "give God back the entrance ticket" to a world in which children suffer.

But at that very moment a sentence came back to me from somewhere deep inside: "Touch the wounds!" And again: *"Put your finger here and see my hands. Reach out your hand and put it in my side. . . ."*

Suddenly there opened up for me once more the story of the apostle Thomas that I had read from John's Gospel at that morning's mass above the tomb of the "patron saint of doubters." Jesus identified with all who are small and suffering. In other words, *all painful wounds and all the human misery in the world are "Christ's wounds."* I can only believe in Christ and have the right to exclaim, "My Lord and my God!" if I touch his wounds, of which our world is still full. Otherwise I say, "Lord, Lord!" simply in vain and to no effect.[11]

Naturally none of us can regard ourselves as a messiah capable of *healing* all the world's wounds. Besides, not even he achieved that during his earthly mission (nor did he attempt to). We must even avoid the temptation (one that often lures to the magic of revolutionary activity) "to turn stones into loaves."[12] Even when we honestly try to do everything that is within our power and capacity, we can only row a short distance against the surging waves of the ocean of poverty that is carving out a larger and larger slice of our continent. Nevertheless, we must not run away from the world's wounds nor turn our backs on them; we have to *see* them at least, touch them and let them involve us. If I remain indifferent to them, uninvolved, unwounded—how can I declare my faith and *love for God, whom I have not seen?*[13] Because at that moment I really do not see God!

Yes, it suddenly became obvious to me there in Madras: I have no right to proclaim belief in God unless I take seriously my neighbor's pain. A faith that would close its eyes to people's suffering is simply an illusion or an opium; both Freud and Marx would be right in criticizing that kind of faith!

But there is also another very important aspect of this: our awareness of suffering in the world must not be restricted solely to "social problems," although that kind of suffering rightly cries out to the conscience of the world and of each of us, and its voice must not be ignored. Nevertheless, we must not for one moment imagine that we have "sorted out" that problem by sending a donation to some charitable operation in Africa or giving alms to a beggar, or voting for political programs with a social emphasis, although these actions are all important. But even that is not enough. There is still much hidden suffering of a different kind inside the people around us. And let us not ignore the unhealed wounds within ourselves—acknowledging and healing them also helps "heal the world"; indeed, it is often a vital prerequisite if we are to be sensitive to the suffering of others and able to help them.

Something else struck me that afternoon in Madras: maybe the doubts of the apostle Thomas were of a different order from the sort that assail us—grandchildren of the age of scientism and positivism—and that we rashly project onto the story. Perhaps the apostle was not simply a maladroit "materialist" incapable of opening himself up to a mystery that he couldn't "touch."

Thomas was a man determined to follow his Master right to the bitter death. Remember how he reacted when Jesus said they had to visit Lazarus: "Let's go and die with him!" He took the cross seriously—and the news of the Resurrection could have seemed to him a meretricious happy end to the Easter story. Maybe that explains why he was reluctant to join in the other apostles' rejoicing and wanted to see Jesus's wounds. He wanted to see for himself that "Resurrection" did not *empty the cross of its meaning*[14] before he could say his "I believe." Did "doubting Thomas" actually understand the meaning of Easter more profoundly than the others?

"The disbelief of Thomas has done more for our faith than the faith of the other disciples," Pope St. Gregory the Great wrote in a homily on this gospel passage.[15]

Jesus comes to Thomas and shows him his wounds: see, no suffering (of any kind) is wiped away and forgotten just like that! Wounds remain wounds. But the one who "bore the ills of us all" passed faithfully through the gates of hell and death; and he continues to be here with us, however hard that is to grasp. He demonstrated that love bears all;[16] "love no flood can quench, no torrents drown," "for love is strong as death,"[17] yea, mightier than death. In the light of that event, love is a value that we must not place at the mercy of sentimentality. It represents a force, the only force that survives death itself and overturns its gates with pierced hands.

So the Resurrection is not a "happy end" but an invitation and a challenge: we ought not, indeed *must* not, capitulate to the fire of suffering, even though we are unable to quench it here and now. In the presence of evil we must not behave as if it should have the last word. Let us not be afraid to "believe in love,"[18] even where it is the loser by the standards of the world. Let us have courage to take our chances with the *folly of the cross* in the face of the "wisdom of this world"![19]

Maybe by resurrecting Thomas's faith through letting him touch the wounds, Jesus was telling him precisely what revealed itself in a flash to me at that Madras orphanage: "It is where you touch human suffering, and maybe only there, that you will realize that I am alive, that 'it's me.' You will meet me wherever people suffer. Do not shy away from me in any of those meetings. Don't be afraid. Do not be unbelieving, but believe!"

The Lord of the Old Covenant appeared to Moses in a burning bush.[20] His only begotten Son, our Lord and our God, appears in the fire of suffering, in the cross—and we make sense of his voice only insofar as we bear our cross and are prepared to bear the loads of others, only insofar as the wounds of the world—his wounds—become a challenge to us.

Without Distance

Each of the apostles was given a task: Peter to care for the sheep of Christ's flock, Paul to travel to distant nations. But what about Thomas?

Let us reflect further on what was alluded to earlier. Being "a believer" does not entail throwing off the burden of agonizing questions forever. Sometimes it means taking upon oneself the cross of doubts and following Jesus faithfully. The strength of faith consists, not of "unshakable conviction," but of the capacity to cope with doubts and ambiguities, to bear the burden of mystery, while maintaining faithfulness and hope.

Yes, maybe that was Thomas's actual mission: the faith that came into being when he touched Jesus's side did not become an object to be "possessed." Even now, faith does not cease to be a *journey* for him. He must continue to bear the burden of his doubts and temptations to skepticism. The certainty of faith comes only when he touches God while touching wounds in the world—only there does he encounter him. There he experiences once more his encounter with the Crucified Christ. Such is his mission.

And that is how, for many who proceed through life in the twilight of doubts, they hack their way through to a totally specific self-revelation of God in our world, to an unexpected "God experience." Those who have seen the Lord open the gates to those who have not: they are able to encounter Jesus over and over again—in the world's wounds.

Those who are unable to find Christ in the traditional surroundings offered by the church, in its preaching, services, and catechisms, still have that opportunity always available to them: to encounter him where people suffer.[1] After all, didn't Jesus say: "Just as you did it to one of the least of these who are members of my family, you did it to me"?[2]

And we can encounter him even in the depths of our own pain.

There are apparently many who have lost their faith in God solely because of the existence of evil and suffering in the world. I must admit that I have never been subject to that temptation. My understanding and experience of it have tended to be quite opposite: almost nothing has aroused in me such a thirst for meaning as the absurdities of the world, and such a thirst for God as the open wounds of life's sorrows.

After all, isn't that intense thirst the earthly form of faith, whereas the radiant certainties and the beatific vision (*visio beatifica*) are reserved for sacred rest in heaven? Faith here on earth is not "certainty" but openness to the Incomprehensible as we ask and seek, occasionally shouting, crying, and protesting, but also as we constantly pray for trust and perseverance, as we have the courage to reject superficial and facile answers and explanations (whether of the atheistic "There is no God!" variety or of the "religious" kind, from those who simply repeat phrases by rote and "right answers" without letting them affect or change their lives). The thirst for God and the question of God rightly conjure up such torrents of associations, imaginings, and related questions (such as the meaning of the word *God* and what *being* might mean in relation to God) that the two dogmatic and categorical answers (the atheistic denial of God and the theistic strait-jacketing of mystery into unequivocal definitions) have always seemed to me equally unfortunate roadblocks before the gates of great spiritual adventure.

If the world were perfect it would already be god, and no question of God would remain in it any longer.[3] A god who gazed narcissistically at the unblemished mirror of his perfect, totally harmonized world in which there were no conflicts, contradictions, or mysteries would not be *my God*, the God of the Bible, the God of my faith. The story told by the Bible is no charming idyll but a disturbing drama. The world about which scripture speaks (like our present-day world) is one of bleeding and painful wounds—and the God that it invokes bears those wounds also.

In the gospel story on which the meditations of this book are based, God appears as a wounded God, not like the apathetic god of the Stoics or god as a projection of our desires, let alone as a symbol of the power ambitions of a man or nation. He is a *sympathetic* God, one who feels *with* us, who suffers *with* us.

Let us now make our first digression into the world of theological thinking.

To speak about a suffering God is always to teeter on the brink of an ancient heresy—Patripassianism, a teaching condemned for claiming that God the Father himself suffered on the cross in Christ. But this claim was rightly condemned because it was a covert expression of another heresy, Monophysitism, which makes no distinction between the Father and the Son or between divinity and humanity in Christ. Rejection of Patripassianism and justified apprehension regarding overanthropomorphic images of God need not lead to the opposite extreme, which is possibly more dangerous, namely, exchanging the God of the Bible for a lifeless pagan concept of divinity, an immobile prime mover, a sort of apathetic and static "supreme being."[4]

Together with the Jews and Muslims we profess belief in a God who is hidden within himself and is revealed in his Word, which *happens* and transforms history. We Christians add to that something that is fundamental for us: the *Word became flesh*—the fullness of that Word, whereby God has been creating the world since the beginning of time and through which he communicates with us people, we distinguish in the man Jesus of Nazareth. He, we maintain, is the Word who was with God in the beginning and was God.[5]

The statement "Jesus is God" sets us apart from Jews and Muslims, who, on account of it, suspect us of betraying monotheism, the pure belief in one God. After years of conversations with Jewish and Muslim theologians I still ask myself the question: Isn't this barrier between us simply a certain interpretation of

Jesus's union with the Father, and not the mystery itself? And could not this mystery—that the man from Nazareth is at one with God in the same way that he is at one with us—express, without the Greek paraphernalia, concepts such as natural behavior, essence, person—mental categories that are not our own by any means? But how otherwise can one talk about that union without its being obvious that this union of the Father and the Son does not diminish either the Father's uniqueness or Jesus's humanity, that it detracts in no way from Jesus's union with us, people, in the same way that that union with us detracts in no way from his unique union with the Father?

Christ is true man and true God—this confession is the be-all and end-all of Christian faith. The teaching of the Council of Chalcedon in antiquity expresses it by the dual use of the expression *homooúsios*—consubstantial—"of one substance" with the Father in his "divine nature." At the same time the personal identity (*prosopon, persona,* person) of Jesus of Nazareth is preserved along with the real difference between the "persons" of the Father and the Son—Jesus is *not* God the Father, Father and Creator of everything and everyone; confessing the unique union of the Father and the Son must not lead to dualism, a weakening of belief in God's singularity and the concomitant belief in the unity and equal dignity of all people (because we are all, in spite of all our differences, equally valuable children of a common Father).

Let us concede, however, that when expressed in that way, the basic Christological dogma, which the early church arrived at after centuries of thrilling intellectual struggles (also suffused unfortunately with personal and political conflict), is a stumbling block not just for Jews and Muslims but also for many Christians. When believers verbally affirm their adherence to this article of faith, their private notions of it are often caricatures that are strongly reminiscent of ancient Christological heresies: Jesus as God clothed as man, Jesus as a hero promoted to divine status, a God-Man, something like a centaur between god and man. . . . It is not surprising that such terrifying chimeras should lead many to resort to a superficially humanistic understanding of Jesus as a "mere" human being, "one of the avatars," or just another teacher of morality, as he is described by those who dilute the strong wine of Christianity beyond recognition with the lukewarm water of relativism, wrongly regarded as the virtue of universal tolerance. What constitutes the Christian confession is not high-minded moral principles of ancient sages but the shocking news that a man born in a stable and put to death in the manner of a rebellious slave should uniquely combine within himself both humanity and divinity (the truth about God and man and their mutual relationship) and that he represents a unique remedy for the deepest wound in "human nature," namely, "salvation" and "the forgiveness of sins." Is it possible to open up to people the depths of the authentic faith of the Christian tradition by attempting to translate the key statements about "the godhead of Christ" and "resurrection" back from the language of metaphysics to the language of narrative?

In fact, there is only one explicit expression of "the godhead of Christ"—and that is precisely when the crucified Christ encounters the "doubting Thomas" and Thomas exclaims, "My Lord and my God!"

Of course the apostle Thomas's declaration "My Lord and my God!" does not constitute a metaphysical definition of Christ's nature. It could be that this joyful exclamation in John's Gospel is not entirely dissimilar to the way the word *god* is used in the Greek of ancient drama. "Recognizing the beloved is god. When friends meet—that is god! God happens!"[6]

Yes, *God happens* also in the Bible, and above all in the Bible. *God is happening.* Thomas discovers in his encounter with the crucified and resurrected Christ that God happens. God is here, "up close." *In the unique Mediator between God and humanity,*[7] God is immediate, at hand, without distance.

In the middle of his *Antichrist*, possibly the most fiercely anti-Christian pamphlet ever written, Nietzsche, "the most devout of the godless" (as he called his Zarathustra), concealed a strange passage, in which, amid the trumpets and drums of his wrath, he surprisingly sings a sonata of his (wounded) love for Jesus. For him, Jesus is "the only Christian who ever lived," and he praises him for demonstrating a relationship between God and humanity "without distance."[8]

It is precisely Jesus's wounds that prove that he lived his solidarity with people "without distance" and that it resulted in his sacrifice on the cross. That is how, in this world, a life of unswerving witness to the truth ends—Jesus's cross is a mirror, in which we see evil and violence in all their nakedness. It is a stark but extremely realistic testimony to the world in which Jesus lived and in which we live too.

"They will look to the one whom they have pierced."[9] Christians have always interpreted this verse of the psalm as prophetic words about the cross. "By his wounds you have been healed," we read elsewhere in scripture.[10] How? Maybe also because we have recognized ourselves in the mirror that the cross and the Crucified placed before the world, and our conversion was motivated by that vision. Maybe we too, who have "clean hands," of course, were awoken from our illusion of innocence and assumed our joint responsibility for the world, whose horrors are caused not only by the actions of wicked people but more often by the indifference and inaction of "good people."

The healing power of the Passion story also resides in the fact that it mirrors not only the world and ourselves but also, in a shocking way, the action of God, who, in his Son, plumbs the very depths of human suffering, finality, and death—*without distance.*

Easter—Pesach, Passover—are festivals commemorating departure. In their celebrations of Pesach, Jews recall the Exodus, the departure from a land of slavery to a promised land of freedom. That is also the fundamental context of the Easter story of Jesus: it is the hour when *he leaves this world and returns to the Father.*[11] It is simultaneously the hour of his enemies' (apparent) victory ("the reign of darkness")[12] and the mysterious feast of Jesus's glorification, as emphasized by John's Gospel, which sees Jesus's *elevation on the cross* simultaneously as his abasement by people and his elevation by the Father "to a place at his right hand."[13]

The Easter narrative as related in John's Gospel begins and ends with two statements: Pilate's exclamation *"Here is the man!"* and Thomas's *"Here is God!"* ("My Lord and my God!"). Both statements refer to Jesus, and both speakers are *looking at his wounds*—one talks about his humanity, the other, his godhead. One could say that the two statements are two different interpretations of Jesus's wounds. His wounds—to a greater degree maybe than anything else, and perhaps they alone—disclose the link between the human and divine that Jesus of Nazareth represents. But what lies between them is the "Easter mystery": Jesus's death and resurrection.

Through his cross, Jesus, who lived his solidarity with people, including with the despised and the uninvited, "without distance," bridged the gulf of sin—the distance between God and people. According to the account on the first pages of the Bible, that distance arose when man ("Adam") was given the choice between trusting or not trusting God and he chose the latter. He accepted a false image of God, a satanically distorted notion of God—God as a begrudging and deceitful competitor of man and his freedom. (In fact, many atheists are rejecting, not the God of the Bible and Christian belief, but this caricature of God proposed by Satan: God fearfully or maliciously preventing the free development of human grandeur. Such rejection is entirely appropriate, for such a perception of God deserves to be rejected; the problem of such atheists is, however, that they have no other concept or experience of God and as a result paradoxically become captive to the error they reject.) Christ's cross is the antithesis of Adam's behavior in the Garden of Eden: whereas Adam's distrust and unfaithfulness destroyed the original Edenic intimacy between man and God, Jesus proves faithful and maintains trust and obedience even in the darkness of forsakenness, which is the fruit and image of the gulf of alienation that scripture designates as "sin."

But let us return to those two sentences that frame the Passion narrative in John's Gospel. Pilate's statement "Here is the man" accompanies the gesture of pointing at a man who has been transformed into a lump of bleeding flesh by vicious scourging. Is it the very same man who was brought that morning before the governor's court as a pretender to the royal throne? Is this still at all a human being? Doesn't his lamentable state in the eyes of the accusers and the crowd of onlookers arouse, if not sympathy, then at least sufficient satisfaction of their bloodlust and desire for punishment, that the governor can finally dismiss this unpleasant lawsuit?

Ecce homo—the scene in which folk piety immerses itself at the beginning of meditation on the stations of the cross and the sorrowful mysteries of the rosary and which is the subject of so many sculptures and paintings—also led the pious imagination further and deeper beyond the superficial meaning of that statement of Pilate's. It is a representation of man, humanity, human existence in extremis, in its weakness, forsakenness, pain, and helplessness, *before which people avert their gaze in horror*;[14] a poor wretch who can say of himself, in the words of the psalm, "I am a worm, and not human; scorned by others, and despised by the people. All who see me mock at me; they make mouths at me, they shake their heads."[15] All glory, power, dignity, and human grandeur are gone; here is humanity as one big bleeding wound. This too is a man!

"Is it nothing to you, all you who pass by? Look and see if there is any sorrow like my sorrow."[16] This is probably why that image, just like the pietà that depicts the mother with the dead son in her lap—the antipode of the Madonna with the child in her arms or in her lap—had such therapeutic power, because it tempered the viewer's own suffering. Jesus on the cross is maybe already too "high," for the cross is often perceived as the culmination of the journey, as a victory ("It is fulfilled"), whereas the scene before Pilate at the beginning of the stations of the cross marks the opening of the drama of pain; the scourging before the tribunal of power and the fanaticism of the crowd is truly the "low point." A man facing the abyss of death, no longer in charge of himself, totally manipulated by the malice of others, delivered entirely into the hands of his enemies, tied with cords like an object, "an unaddressed parcel," which the Sanhedrin, Pilate, Herod, the soldiers, and the executioners pass back and forth between each other—this image illustrates the lowest point of human existence, stripped of all embellishment and all support.

Here is the man! Pilate's earlier sentence, the question "What is truth?,"[17] was similarly cryptic. Maybe it was just a cynically derisory comment by a political pragmatist ("Truth—what's that? What does it matter?"), made without a trace of philosophical curiosity. Jesus's response is silence. But isn't the *Ecce homo* the real answer?

The man covered in wounds expresses a profound truth about man and his fate. Man is *nothing*—that is the truth of Good Friday, without which there is no Easter morning. Only where there are graves are there resurrections[18]—even on this point old Nietzsche was right. What do we know about man so long as we avoid the possibility of looking without illusions at the absolute limits of human destiny, if we don't plumb the depths and if we avert our gaze from the abyss?

Suffice it to recall the brilliant analysis of the relationship between truth, power, and violence in the works of Michel Foucault. In the scene before Pilate we are confronted with truth located entirely outside the realm of power and violence, truth that found its place in human powerlessness and that explicitly abjured violence. ("If my kingdom were from this world, my followers would be fighting to keep me from being handed over to the Jews," Jesus tells Pilate.)[19] Rather than joining forces with violence, rather than committing violence or responding with violence and thus endlessly breeding violence, truth becomes its victim. Its voluntary sacrifice reveals the essence of violence and seeks thereby—with all the consequences involved—to block the unleashed mechanism of vengeance that demands more and more victims.[20] It cannot "stop" the mechanism but can show its true nature and become a challenge to those who will understand its sacrifice as a way of refusing to support the mechanism, to collaborate with it and employ its methods.

If Jesus is God's word for us, the word that assumed humanity in entirety, then his humanity embraces not only the grandeur and perfection of man as a still-incorrupt image of God (he is the new Adam, Adam unscarred by the Fall) but also its antithesis, the dark, scarred aspect of the human condition—destitution and wretchedness from which we would rather avert our gaze, stop our ears, and close our hearts.

Aren't we, who were born in the century when human beings shed many of the illusions of modern humanism on the appelplatzes of Nazi and communist concentration camps, we who live in a millennium on whose very threshold many nascent optimistic hopes and expectations of "bright tomorrows" were violently massacred by the terrorist attack of September 11, 2001, challenged by that historical experience to examine afresh the *Ecce homo* scene and gain a deeper understanding of it? Don't we feel a greater affinity and familiarity with a wounded defendant being tried under a cynical regime than with the bucolic and schmaltzy images of a smiling "Good Shepherd"?

Pascal was already fully aware that a religion afraid to point out people's wretchedness to them is simply the self-deception of narcissistic projection: *"Those who have known God, without knowing their wretchedness, have not glorified him, but have glorified themselves."*[21]

At the end of the Easter story according to John, Jesus's wounds are once more on display, and the apostle who has previously been racked by doubt exclaims: My Lord and my God!

Easter is an exodus—the shift from one view of Jesus's wounds to another, a shift from *"Ecce homo!"* to *"Ecce Deus!"* What the church traditionally expresses in metaphysical language as "two natures" we can call two ways of interpreting Jesus's wounds. Jesus's wounds seen from two points of view elicit two reactions, clothed in two words—*man* and *God.* And these words, so radically distinct (but profoundly linked, of course), can refer to one and the same person.

Neither Pilate nor Thomas is making a theological statement about the "natures" of Jesus. Both are expressing powerful emotion or an emotional experience of encounter.

Thomas's exclamation is generally understood to be the amazement and joy of a man whose senses have convinced him about the physical reality of the Resurrection. As I have intimated, maybe there could be more to it. (What the wise rabbis maintained about Torah texts applies equally to the New Testament, namely that every place in the Bible is so profound that it permits at least seventy different interpretations.)[22] Thomas's joy, his "second conversion," was brought about by something that seems to have affected him more than the other apostles: unity in Christ—the oneness of the crucified and the resurrected Jesus. Jesus's wounds were the evidence for that.

It is clear from all the accounts of encounters with the resurrected Christ that he was radically changed by his passage through the "valley of the shadow of death." Neither the disciples traveling to Emmaus nor even Mary Magdalene, who was so close to him, recognized him immediately. The Gospels apparently seek to emphasize that the Resurrection mystery is a radical transformation, not a mere reanimation of a corpse (resuscitation) and return to this world and this life.

Mary Magdalene recognized him by his voice, the disciples on the road to Emmaus by his gesture when breaking bread, Thomas by his wounds. What Jesus uses to identify himself—first to his disciples gathered at supper behind locked doors, and then, more distinctly and with greater urgency to Thomas—are his wounds, an *anamnesis* (a reminiscence or reminder) of the cross. Jesus enters "through a closed door," overcoming the apostles' fearful reclusion and showing them "his hands and his side."

Later, Thomas, on seeing Jesus's wounds, can experience the fulfillment of his words: "Whoever has seen me has seen the Father."[23] He sees God in Jesus—and sees him through the chasm of his wounds.

Maybe not only the *oneness* of the crucified and resurrected Jesus but also the mysterious union of godhead and humanity—which is expressed by that Chalcedonian dogma (about the godhead of Christ, and Jesus truly God and truly man), which for many is a stumbling block—is glimpsed through Jesus's wounds.

I said earlier that in Thomas's encounter God not only becomes apparent but actually *happens*. God does not come to people as a "fact," a "given," "an object" that can be "grasped," understood, and owned. In his inspirational book *The God Who May Be*,[24] the outstanding contemporary Irish philosopher Richard Kearney (who now works mostly in the US) suggests a third possibility between the fundamentalist theist concept of God as "a given" and the similarly fundamentalist assertion of atheists that "there is no God"—namely, that *God may be*. God addresses people (such as Moses from the burning bush)[25] as a possibility, he presents himself as a proposition, a challenge, a task (e.g., "Go and free my people."). In that dialogue God happens, he *becomes real* where people accept his appeal (and him as the one making the appeal).

It is remarkable how God generally addresses people on the margins or in distress. (Moses is a fugitive, tending the flocks of his father-in-law.) Jesus—and God in Jesus—not only shows solidarity with them (the small, the uninvited, the wounded—what we spoke about in the previous chapter) but actually identifies with them: just as you did not do it to one of the least of these, you did not do it to *me*.[26]

"No one can come to the Father except through me."[27] Christian fundamentalists and "exclusivists" love to quote these words of Jesus. It is used by these self-appointed guardians of the gates of the heavenly kingdom to turn the name of Jesus into a shibboleth to easily identify and exclude those who are rejected from the outset. And yet, as Kearney points out, they have typically forgotten to ask themselves who that sentence is about, who constitutes Jesus's "me": Who and where is Jesus, the only Mediator between us and the Father? "Who am I?" Jesus answered this question, didn't he, when he declared, "Just as you did not do it to one of the least of these, you did not do it to *me*." The least, people on the fringes (and on the fringes of the church), the needy (not only socially), the wounded (not only physically), are the sure and only path to the Father that cannot be relativized or circumvented. Jesus himself is here with them and in them as the way, the truth, and the life.

Jesus is everywhere that there are the needy—and for us they are everywhere (and he in them) as an "opportunity," as an open gate to the Father. And where is Jesus not to be found? In just one place: namely, in those and with those who consider themselves to be righteous and far-sighted, who exclude others and turn Jesus's words into a bar for the gate, which they meticulously guard. They themselves cannot enter, and they prevent others from entering.

This interpretation of Jesus's "No one can come to the Father except through me" is not an attempt to relativize Jesus's role or undermine his claim to exclusivity and thrust Christ back into the anonymous ranks of an orderless multitude. On the contrary, we accept him in his fullness (with everything in which he reveals and gives himself). It is that fullness that constitutes the mystery of his uniqueness—in exactly the way that his uniqueness resides in the mystery of his unique union with the Father.

Arcanum Cordis

"The secret of his heart is laid open through the clefts of his body" (Patet arcanum cordis per foramina corporis), wrote the saintly mystic Bernard de Clairvaux.[1] I confess that for a number of reasons it took a long while for me to summon up the courage to write about this *arcanum*—it is "too great a mystery"; it is truly *mysterium tremendum et fascinans*, a mystery that fascinates but also causes us to tremble in awe. Two paths lead to it—the broad path of several ancient Easter observances and the steep path of the theologians, philosophers, and mystics (or rather theologians who were also philosophers and mystics). Both paths have their great pitfalls.

Popular veneration of the Five Holy Wounds, the Most Sacred Heart, Our Lady of Sorrows, the Seven Last Words of Christ, the Veil of Veronica, the Turin Shroud, the Stations of the Cross, the Sorrowful Mystery of the Rosary, this all has the capacity either to initiate the believer into the deeper meaning of the Easter story or to remain at the level of externals and stay mired in the shallows of the sentimental weepers that Jesus chided on the way to his crucifixion ("Daughters of Jerusalem, do not weep for me, but weep for yourselves and for your children"),[2] when not actually sinking into a poisonous mire of sadomasochistic fantasy. (Can all those pious practices be said to have boosted opposition to violence in the Christian world and encouraged solidarity with its victims? Did not, time and again, Christian mobs rush off to plunder Jewish ghettos immediately on hearing the story of the Passion, instead of beating their breasts in contrition? Did not many Christians, after centuries of repeated Easter celebrations, remain passive and even unconcerned at the time of the greatest anti-Jewish pogrom in human history—Auschwitz—that "Golgotha of the modern world," in the words of John Paul II?)

And where do the paths of the philosophers and theologians lead? I really am not superstitious, but I shudder somewhat when I think about the odd coincidence of this particular theme and the fate of those who probably delved most deeply into the mystery of the cross and the death of God-man. Nietzsche, who circled moth-like around the stupendous mystery of the "death of God," was eventually scorched by the flame of madness. The Protestant Dietrich Bonhoeffer and the Jesuit Alfred Delp, who, with their gaze on the cross of Christ, addressed the tragic aspects of the faith perspective and also faith without the support of a metaphysical image of God, both died on the scaffold before consummating their ideas. Edith Stein, the philosopher and Carmelite nun of Jewish origin (St. Teresa Benedicta of the Cross), did not complete her work "The Science of the Cross" but was murdered on that "Calvary of our times" in the gas chamber at Auschwitz. The Czech philosopher Jan Patočka, who was convinced that "Christianity is an unfinished project" and who, at underground seminars, in response to our pressing questions, said simply that in his view theologians had not yet given sufficient thought to the sentence "My God, why have you forsaken me?," never did finish penning or voicing those ideas; at the same age as Socrates he abandoned academic seclusion and entered the political and moral arena, dying after repeated secret-police interrogations. Like Socrates, he fell victim to the malice of those who reproached him for "failing to acknowledge the gods that the city acknowledges and corrupting the youth." And there are undoubtedly many more such instances.

It is as if those ideas were kept from being fully expounded, as if they had to remain simply suggested—and be fully expounded not on paper or in university precincts but in a place where the cross cast its shadow over human destinies; as if, at a given moment, those thinkers, like the apostle Paul, *had to complete, through their suffering, what was lacking in Christ's afflictions,*[3] whose dark depths had been the object of their meditations. Or had precisely those meditations given some of them the motivation and strength to undergo a life change in the direction of "nonindifference" (which is one of the names of faith),[4] the courage to sacrifice themselves and to "carry a cross" in a real sense?

Let us rather return to those popular forms of piety mentioned earlier and take them as our starting point!

For centuries on Easter Saturday (sometimes known as Bright or Holy Saturday) at the end of Easter Week, hordes of people (none of whom had read Nietzsche's reflections on the "death of God") unhesitatingly made their way to the "Tomb of God" (and they continue to do so unless the "Tomb of God" has been abolished because of some rather punctilious interpretation of postconciliar liturgical reform), in order to silently venerate the "holy wounds."

At this point we must make a second digression into theological history and theological thinking. The entirely orthodox use of the expression "Tomb of God" (and hence also "the death of God") gives Christians access to a remarkable component of the treasury of theological tradition, namely, the doctrine of *communicatio idiomatum* (the communication of properties). In order to emphasize the unity of divinity and humanity in Christ and the interrelationship of the persons of the triune God (*perichoresis*), we may—in a precisely defined sense—use the characteristics applied to God the Father with respect to the Son and vice versa. Thus we may say that "God died" when we seek to express that the person who died was simultaneously God and man, even though—which we must bear in mind at the same time—he died "in his human but not in his divine nature." These reflections may seem somewhat cumbersome, but the principle of *communicatio idiomatum* is an excellent hermeneutic key for interpreting the paradoxes of Christian faith, and above all it enables the use of magnificently poetic language in theology, the liturgy, preaching, and Christian art. Without it the pithy language of the German mystics would not have evolved—particularly that of Meister Eckhart—and of their radical successor Martin Luther with his theology of the cross, based on the idea that the hidden God appears only *sub contrario*: as the opposite of God. And what would be left, for instance, of the fascinating dynamic of Baroque art without that interplay of light and shade, the constant intermingling of colorful sensuality and spiritual ecstasy, the azure sky and the scarlet flames from the throat of hell! What language would the great thinkers of Christianity, such as Pascal or Kierkegaard, have spoken as a religion of paradox? What would be left of the paradoxes of sin and grace in the novels of Graham Greene? "Death of God theology," that modern heir of Paul's and Luther's *theology of the cross*, would be reduced to a mixture of absurdities and blasphemy—as indeed that school is regarded by those who would like to turn theology into a somewhat pedantic "science" and who have never been initiated into the *art* of thinking theologically!

Let us now follow those who came to "the Tomb of God" on Easter Saturday to venerate the "holy wounds"—the wounds of God. What are Christ's wounds? What is that wound in his heart, revealing, through the wounded body, the *arcanum*, his innermost mystery? What is the most inherent pain, distress, and darkness of the cross? It is not the physical torment that pietism so delighted in, nor yet physical death itself. It is something else, something profounder and more appalling. To touch Christ's wounds, not only those in his hands and feet, which tell of his physical suffering, but also "the wound in his side" that struck the heart, is to touch the darkness contained in the cry of one totally abandoned by God. That wound in the heart is what is testified to by Jesus's words on the cross that only one of the evangelists had the courage to preserve: *My God, why have you forsaken me?*[5]

In that sentence we already glimpse the darkness of the moment of which the Apostles' Creed speaks: he descended into hell.[6] One is tempted to say (if, in spite of all the license that the language of preaching enjoys thanks to *communicatio idiomatum*, one were not afraid to step onto that thin footbridge over the yawning abyss of blasphemy) that at that moment his faith and his union with the

Father were crucified and pierced, that at that moment for him (and in him) "God died": Jesus took upon himself not just human death but also the *death of God*.

If there is any "Christian meaning" to the sentence "God is dead," which has fascinated the West for over a century, if it has some kind of *locus theologicus*, then it is in the mystery of Good Friday and also in the abyss opened by the cry of the Crucified.

Tradition teaches us that Jesus drained the bitter cup of separation from God. To be alone and alienated from God, when God seems remote and silent, totally absent, even dead, is not just the consequence of sin or punishment for sin but the mysterious essence of sin, its dark heart. Grave "mortal" sin kills the life of grace in us, as every catechism tells us. And now God and sin encounter each other as never before—at a given moment these two radical opposites are interlaced and interfused: he became sin for us,[7] says St. Paul about the crucified Christ. Martin Luther developed the idea dramatically: God commanded him, the only righteous one, to become the greatest sinner, to descend into all the sins of the world, to be the transgressor in Adam, the murderer in Cain, the adulterer in David, the coward in Peter, the traitor in Judas. . . . What wasn't accepted could not be redeemed!

To be a sacrificial lamb and take upon oneself all the sins of the world, as Paul profoundly understood it, amounts to extreme solidarity with sinners, the most extreme possible: not *to sin* but to *become sin*. That is the mystery of the cross, the paradox of the confrontation between sin and God in a human heart, which is simultaneously the heart of God, in the human heart of the man from Nazareth, about which the church sings in the Litany of the Sacred Heart of Jesus, using Paul's words: "in whom dwells the fullness of divinity." It is that instant in the age-old battle between good and evil, that dizzying moment of death when time plunges into eternity, when evil, sin, violence, darkness, and death seemed on the verge of victory. That instant when the attack on God, which was and is sin (Adam's attempt to be "like God" and thus render God superfluous—and all of our sins, which are simply a ratification of that displacement of God), seemed to have succeeded.

G. K. Chesterton recommended Christ as "the God of atheists": if atheists were to choose their religion, they should choose Christianity, for in it "God seemed for an instant to be an atheist."[8]

Isn't that *arcanum*, the closely guarded mystery that can be glimpsed through the wound in the heart of God the Son, that total "divine self-denial," as if God divested himself of his being and hid within that *nothing* that all creatures, all *mortals* must traverse? Isn't that the crucial moment in the everlasting dialogue between the Father and the Son, and the dialogue of the Creator with the world and humanity—that God in the suffering of his Son fulfilled his solidarity with us in our pettiness and mortality, to the extent of concealing his face from his Son, as well as his entire being, so that even the Son at that moment experienced him as a *totally absent* "dead" God?

However, is not the Son's redeeming and liberating act when, even at that moment of total darkness, he *does not falter*, but voices that "crucified faith" in his dying cry, expressing that most extreme of experiences not in the language of despair and resignation but in the form of an agonizing question?

If his faith was "crucified" and pierced by the experience of God's infinite remoteness, for which we have no grimmer expression than "the death of God," then the very fact that Jesus voices that extreme experience in the form of a question, "*Why* have you abandoned me?," that he does not cease asking, that he *continues to dialogue* with the Father, when, in his death throes, he can no longer expect any answer, is in human terms a portent of the Resurrection. That moment before which, according to the Gospels, even the sun hid its face already carries within it the dawn of the Easter morning. John rightly portrays the cross also as a victory, Christ's humiliation as "exaltation," and instead of the dreadful question of the Abandoned One, he already hears the peace and reconciliation (*shalom*) of the victorious morning that is approaching: It is finished!

Considering that at the moment when Jesus feels totally abandoned by God, his cry—*in spite of everything*—is a *question*, this moment of the cross (and the cross of his faith, if we put it that way) reveals something fundamental about the character of a truly *Christian* (not a "universally religious") faith in general: the authentic faith of Jesus's disciples is faith "in spite of everything," faith "regardless"; it is a faith that is wounded, pierced, yet *constantly questioning* and seeking—one that is crucified and resurrected; in other words, a truly Easter faith.

A Torn Veil

According to the Gospel of Matthew, at the moment of Jesus's death the veil of the Temple was torn in two,[1] and the Holy of Holies of the Temple of Jerusalem was revealed in all its naked-ness, darkness, and emptiness. The open and empty tabernacles in Catholic churches on Holy Saturday are a reminder of two pro-foundly connected symbols—the unveiled Holy of Holies of the Temple and Jesus's heart, opened by the Roman centurion's lance.

Jesus's heart is also empty now—according to the Gospel of John, blood and water flowed out of it, perceived in the commen-taries of the church fathers as a foretoken of the sacraments of bap-tism and the Eucharist.[2] God's suffering servant did indeed "empty himself."[3] Like the emptiness of the Holy of Holies, Jesus's open-ness and emptiness express that mysterious coalescence of empti-ness and fullness that, for thousands of years, has fascinated mystics of not only Western but above all Eastern spiritual paths.

The piercing of the heart and rending of the veil (the epistle to the Hebrews speaks of the curtain as a body)[4] is also a tearing down of the wall of enmity between God and people, and between people themselves. Now everyone who takes the path indicated by the arms of the Crucified will be able to enter by "the new and living path to the Holy of Holies," to the Father of all, irrespective of nation, cul-ture, or language. *He is our peace*[5] (*shalom*), our reconciliation, Paul constantly repeats; there is no longer any "us" or "them." Concern-ing the space opened by the cross, the Croatian Protestant theolo-gian Miroslav Volf wrote:

> At the heart of the cross is Christ's stance of not letting the other remain an enemy and of creating space in himself for

the offender to come in. Read as the culmination of the larger narrative of God's dealing with humanity, the cross says that despite its manifest enmity toward God humanity belongs to God. . . . The cross is the giving up of God's self in order not to give up on humanity; it is the consequence of God's desire to break the power of human enmity without violence and receive human beings into divine communion. . . . The arms of the crucified are open—a sign of a space in God's self and an invitation for the enemy to come in.[6]

The tearing of the Temple veil was seen as the fulfillment, that is, the end, of "the old covenant" and its replacement by a new and eternal covenant, sealed in the blood of the cross of Jesus. The Lord's original covenant with the chosen people is thus transcended by the new openness of God's heart; henceforth it extends to all nations and applies to all people.[7] Jesus fulfills the role of Temple, High Priest, and temple sacrifice. He is the sole High Priest for all time, henceforth the one and only Mediator between God and people; he himself is the true, living Temple, he himself is the sacrifice that fulfills, supersedes, and continues to invalidate all former sacrificial rituals.[8] Not through the blood of goats and calves, but through a "new and living way" opened for us by Christ with his own blood, "through the veil, that is, his body," can we now draw near to God.[9] That was how it was already understood by the first generations of Christians, and that understanding is also evident in the New Testament letters, and particularly in the theology of the Letter to the Hebrews.

The veil of the Temple was said to be interwoven with stars and constellations to symbolize the universe.[10] So the tearing of the veil (like the piercing of Jesus's heart) acquires a further meaning: it indicates the cosmic dimension of Jesus's redemptive sacrifice. The philosophers of the golden age of late German metaphysics, Schelling and particularly Hegel, wrote about the significance of the cross and "the death of God" for the history of the absolute Spirit, encompassing the entire history of nature and mankind; during the previous centuries, Easter hymns in the breviary had sung about the blood in which the stars themselves were washed.

When the priest consecrates the paschal candle in the liturgy on the eve of the Easter vigil, before he prays, "By his holy and glorious wounds may Christ our Lord guard and keep us," he embeds into the candle five gilded grains of incense symbolizing Christ's five transformed and healing wounds, using them to inscribe the first and last letters of the Greek alphabet in remembrance of the cosmic greatness of the Risen One, encompassing time and space: *Christ yesterday and today, the beginning and the end, Alpha and Omega, all time belongs to him. . . .*

For centuries Christians probably thought little about how the mystique of the torn veil must have hurt the Jews—their older brothers and sisters in faith. Doesn't the tearing of the veil mean the invalidation of Judaism—and doesn't that idea imply that Jews as Jews (unless they convert to Christianity) have no further raison d'être? And isn't it just a small step from this idea (which fortunately remains largely half-baked) to the passivity with which many Christians looked on (or turned away) when the anti-Jewish and anti-Christian neopaganism of Nazism tried to implement its "final solution"—the erasure of Jews and Judaism from history? Were there not also at the time Christians who saw even in the Holocaust (as well as in the destruction of the Jerusalem Temple by the Nazis nearly twenty centuries earlier) the merited fulfillment of the words of the Jewish accusers in response to Pilate's judgment as recorded in Matthew's Gospel: "His blood be on us and on our children!"?

When we Catholics hear nowadays from many quarters (particularly in Czechia) how the *present-day* church continues to be blamed for the real sins of the medieval church (or for those transgressions fabricated or exaggerated by Enlightenment and Marxist historians), and are surprised that people around us fail to see the absurdity of ascribing to us something that we Christians of today truly have nothing to do with (indeed, many of us would be more likely to have been victims of the Inquisition, rather than Inquisitors or executioners), we should remind ourselves that only a few generations ago many Christians considered it normal to apply this historically absurd assumption of "collective guilt" to the Jews. Did it really take a Nazi Holocaust for papal documents to declare plainly that responsibility for the alleged behavior of the Sanhedrin two millennia ago could not be attributed to the entire Jewish nation at the time of Jesus, let alone today?

In one of his articles, one of the most significant representatives of Catholic "post-Auschwitz" theology, Johann B. Metz, recalls in one of his articles that the synagogue in the portal of Bamberg Cathedral is depicted as a drooping blindfolded woman alongside a triumphantly upright woman symbolizing the church. (The motif of two women, the church and the synagogue, in which the synagogue, in a reference to Paul's text about the veil in the hearts of the Jews who did not accept Christ,[11] is depicted blindfolded, is frequently found in the portals of Gothic cathedrals.) And Metz asks: *What do you think those blindfolded eyes might have seen?*[12]

In opposition to the heretic Marcion of Sinope, the early church decided definitively in the second century after Christ that it would always honor the Hebrew Bible as part of its Holy Scripture, so we should also thereby feel obliged to regard the memory of the Jews—from Abraham up to the present time—including the wounds inflicted or tolerated by Christians, as a sacred part of our own memory. When we profess in the creed our belief in the "community of saints" (*communio sanctorum*), we must not exclude from it or disregard "God's first love"—Israel. Yes, our "solidarity with victims" to which, according to Metz, we are committed by Jesus's cry on the cross must include not only those who wear a cross on their chest but also those who have worn there the Star of David.

Metz recalls the description of Israel as "a landscape of screams."[13] Instead of presenting people with comforting myths to "explain" their suffering (plenty of which can be found in the mythology of surrounding nations), the psalmist and the prophets allow these voices of the sufferers to resound before God, to call for final, eschatological justice, or (which amounts to the same thing) the hour of the Messiah's arrival. Hence Metz views the message of the Resurrection as a promise that God heard his Son's cry of pain and embraced the lamentation of those who were denied a voice in history "written by the victors"; Metz therefore implores Christians always to include the cry of the Crucified in their preaching about the Resurrection, since otherwise it would simply present the "mythology of the victor" and not the Christian theology of the cross.

Now that our meditation on the "Tomb of God" has led us to these reflections on Israel, let us ask whether the theme of the "silence" and "absence" of God, which imbues the Christian experience of "Holy Saturday," is also to be found in "Jewish memory" and Jewish theology.

When I first stood at the Western Wall, the "Wailing Wall" of the Temple in Jerusalem destroyed by the Romans in 70 AD, I became aware of the similarity between this unique "monument" and the Tomb of God of Holy Saturday, and how in fact, in a certain sense—in the spirit of "negative (apophatic) theology"—it reveals the essence of religious metaphor and symbolism in general: this place is holy because *it refers to what is not there*—and thus enables one to experience the painful absence of the One who is Present, and also the comforting mysterious presence of the One who is Absent.

Since time immemorial, "divine hiddenness" has been a theme of Jewish thought and particularly of Jewish mysticism, the Kabbalah. Maybe the Kabbalistic idea of "divine contraction" could be regarded as an expression of God's hiddenness.[14] God is omnipresent, so when God was creating the world and human beings, a space must have been created within God for the world. The designation of God's presence as *Shekinah*, which accompanied God's people even in exile, can be seen as another expression of God's hiddenness. The Jews link God's exile with the difficult moments of their history—*Shekinah* suffers with the Jews the years of slavery in Egypt and also shares with them the hardships of their journey through the desert; it accompanies the exiled Jews to Babylon and shares with them the loss of their homeland and their dispersal among the nations. Indeed, the greatest development of the Kabbalah is linked to the dark hour of the Jews' history in the Middle

Ages, when they were exiled from Spain; in this teaching the Jewish scholars at Safed in Palestine were certainly seeking an answer to those events.

Jewish "post-Auschwitz theology"—after the terrifying experience of "God's silence" and God's absence and failure to intervene—once more revived that ancient theme: according to Hans Jonas, God gave up one of his attributes, his omnipotence. God was present in Auschwitz in those who did not cease to pray even there, or who, like Job, called for justice.[15] God is now present in the world only through the prayer, hope, and faithfulness of those who worship God, and through their response to God's Word; but they need to become listeners in order to hear it.

The words of Elie Wiesel, who returns continually in his novels and essays to the religious meaning of his own experience of Auschwitz (although on each occasion he comes to the conclusion that he cannot understand it), have a familiar ring and are a source of inspiration to the Christian who reflects on Jesus's struggle in Gethsemane and on his cry on the cross, and God's silence, the silence of Holy Saturday (and on everything foreshadowed and symbolized by those Easter themes). "I do not believe that we can talk about God; we can only—as Kafka said—talk to God. It depends on who is talking. What I try to do is speak to God. Even when I speak against God, I speak to God. And even if I am angry at God, I try to show God my anger. But even that is a profession, not a denial of God."[16] And one of the commentators on Wiesel's writings comments: "To quarrel with God is to pay God the supreme compliment: it is to take God seriously. . . . To be indifferent to God is to pay God the supreme insult. It is to say that nothing of consequence is at stake. . . . There are a number of concerns that justify 'the shout [that] becomes a prayer.' When there is manifest evil in the world, the shout is morally necessary. . . . In defense of creation, on behalf of humanity—even for the sake of God may human contention against God be justified."[17]

Even when the veil of the Temple is torn, even when the Temple is burnt down and destroyed, even when God is silent, humans (not only in their loyal obedience but also in their questioning and anger) do not remain indifferent to God.

The God about whom the Bible speaks is revealed in God's work, in God's creation, and above all in the incarnation of God's Son. Nevertheless—as the great Christian theologians emphasize—what God is "in God's self," and "as God *is*" (what the verb *to be* means if it is applied to God's being), remains for us an incomprehensible mystery. God's hiddenness has also been emphasized by Christian *negative theology*. In that tradition Meister Eckhart wrote: "God . . . is a not-God, a not-Spirit, a not-Person." In other words, God is not "a being" among other beings in the world—in this world of material things God is "no-thing"—and you, human being, must become "nothing" (not be fixated on anything in this world, and not identify with anything, but remain "poor"—i.e., inwardly free), if you want to meet God ("naked with the naked Godhead"). Only in such "nothingness" (poverty and freedom) can one be "God's equal."

Martin Luther, who, in many respects, drew on this negative theology, linked the idea of the total hiddenness and inaccessibility of God with the "theology of the cross," thus radically expanding on the teaching of St. Paul. God is revealed through God's antithesis (*sub contrario*); God is concealed in paradoxes. It is pointless to seek God through God's hidden essence, his power, divinity, or goodness. That is the (vain) striving of philosophers and (false) "theologians of glory." It is impossible to rely on reason and philosophy (or, similarly, on one's deeds, merits, or goodwill)—these are just the devil's will-o'-the-wisps on the path to God. The only real Christian theologian is the theologian of the cross, who knows that there is no other path to knowing God than the path to the power of God concealed in his weakness, in the humiliation and powerlessness of the Crucified One; than the path to the beauty of God, hidden in the horrifying ugliness of God's wounds; than the path to God's justice, revealed in the one who became sin for us. The path to God's tender and merciful love leads solely through its hiddenness in the cruel drama of Easter. The encounter with God almost always happens "in a place, at a time, in a manner, and through the agency of such a person, at such a place and in such a manner as we do not think possible . . . because he is near to us and in us, simply in a unfamiliar form, not in the radiance of his glory, but in lowliness and meekness so one might think it is not him; but it really is."[18] According to Luther, we must replace neo-Platonic and Scholastic attempts to speak about God from the perspective of eternity, *sub specie aeternitatis*, with a view of God *sub specie temporis*, in other words, from our human perspective. We have to disregard "God in his majesty and his nature" because we have nothing to do with such a God; we have simply been given *Deus humanus,* revealed in Christ and his cross. But this *Deus humanus* is the very antithesis of the pious notions and wishes of our reason.

There is also a terrifying aspect to Luther's concealed God: "He stands behind all the terrible and appalling things that happen, all the absurdities of history." He dons *"the mask of the devil"* and can *"escape into total absence." "It is necessary to seek protection from this hidden God (Deus absconditus) in the revealed God (Deus revelatus) and flee from God to God."*[19]

Discovering such a hidden and surprising God, and agreeing with the scandalous and crazy statement that the accursed Crucified is alive once more and that the source of salvation is entirely beyond the scope of reason, is something that only courage and the grace of faith can achieve. One cannot accede to "God's self," the naked God (*Deus nudus*); the attempts of metaphysicians to grasp the essence of God as an abstraction are more a revelation of human pettiness and nakedness (*homo nudus*), if not actually a direct path into the devil's maw. For us God is *Deus humanus.*

There is similarly no point in speculating about Christ's "nature" instead of concerning ourselves with what God means *for us,* and the riches (*beneficia Christi*) with which God endows us. God clothes us—our sinfulness and nakedness—in the mantle of Christ's blood, as a mantle of righteousness, and declares us righteous. On the basis of Christ's victory over death, which is the death of death (*mors mortis*), every Christian is now a sinner and one of the righteous at one and the same time (*simul iustus et peccator*). Not for a single moment did Luther's sense of paradox abandon him in his teaching about God and salvation.

Few have probably understood and radically developed "Paul's gospel"—the most profound and unique contribution of the New

Testament—as incisively as those thinkers of paradox: Luther, Pascal, and Kierkegaard.

The cross is a judgment on all other gods and powers that might seek to wrap themselves in the aura of divinity and offer salvation—they will all disappear like nocturnal phantasms and shadows when banished by the light of faith. I can therefore permit myself to admit all the doubts, all the "critiques of religion," and all the truths of critical atheism, and the truth of "religion" as a human invention and as a projection of our desires and fears, Karl Barth declared, following Luther's logic. According to him, faith, which opens itself to God's Word and is our salvation in Jesus and his cross, is the complete opposite of religion, which seeks (in vain—foolishly and blasphemously) to climb to God up the ladder of its own theological constructions, pious fantasies, or other intellectual or moral achievements or merits.

I don't expect Catholic theology will ever fully share the pathos of all those passionate Protestant *sola*—"only" (only by faith, only by grace, only by scripture, only by the cross); the Catholic principle is "not only but also" (God is revealed not only in scripture but also in tradition, not only in grace but also in freedom of conscience and will, not only in the cross but also in creation). But if Christian theology is truly to be catholic (i.e., universal, entire, all-embracing), if it is truly to live up to the principle of compatibility of apparent contradictions ("not only but also"), then it must also not fear these dramatic notes and close itself off from them; instead it must be capable of listening attentively to their profundity and truth. Torn out of the entirety of the tradition (primarily the one he grew out of, i.e., not only Paul but also Augustine, and chiefly the German mystics), Luther would truly be seductively one-sided; but perceived in the broad context of the tradition, he is not only a great theologian but deservedly a fascinating preacher, poet, and mystic of the cross, akin to the Spanish mystics of the early Baroque period.[20]

In a certain sense, the "death of God theology" of the 1960s was chiefly a radicalization of Luther's theology of the cross, or the theme of the "paradox of the cross" to be found in St. Paul and Tertullian, as well as in Pascal and Kierkegaard. (Indeed, Nietzsche—as Dietrich von Hildebrand once pointed out—was, in a certain sense, a "radically Protestant preacher," and his statement "God is dead" can be taken as a kind of offshoot of the "negative theology" of Eckhart and the German mystics, and of Luther's "theology of the cross.") This "theology of the death of God" was a bit of a premature baby; it arrived too late to take up the gauntlet thrown down to Christianity by Nietzsche, and too soon to confront the challenges of our age, when radical secularism rubs shoulders with an overabundance of intrusive tawdry religiosity and esotericism.[21]

Only now are we once more profoundly confronted in Europe by the mystery of Holy Saturday: on the surface, in "naked public space," the inquisitors of political correctness decree silence of the grave about God (*magnum silentium est in terra*, we read in the breviary about Holy Saturday), while "in the depths" ferocious combat is taking place over the essentials (*mors et vita duello*).

The phrase "God is dead" seems to be regarded by some authors simply as a more radical version of the idea of God's inaccessibility (and God's concealment in the cross of Christ), expressed first by Luther and certain mystics. But others go even further: God took on humanity, solidarizing and identifying so much with humankind, and "being emptied" so much, that God really died on the cross of Christ—and now, as Thomas Altizer maintained, God is here solely in the form of mankind and its history.

Some of the "death of God theologians"—again clearly in Luther's footsteps—propose replacing the old wording of "Jesus is God" with another assertion, "God is Jesus": God is with us in Jesus and the "humanity for others" lived by Jesus. If "God has gone on a journey" (as we read in several of Jesus's parables), then God left a "deputy"—the Son, who performs God's work, plays God's role, takes over God's cause: he consoles those who don't understand God and were left hungry by God, Dorothee Sölle writes. And this deputy calls on his own deputies—us—to serve as "witnesses to the truth."

Remember Rolf Hochhuth's controversial play *The Deputy*. Its hero is a Jesuit who protests against the silence of the then pope ("Christ's deputy") about Nazi persecution by voluntarily wearing a yellow star and going off to a concentration camp as a "representative" of Christ's official deputy and, by so doing, becomes a true "deputy of Christ."[22]

One interpretation of the phrases "God is dead" and "God has died" maintains that these statements express the experience that previous talk about God—indeed, the very word *God*—is now meaningless. It might be possible to discover God again—but only by looking at Christ. Old talk about God has become incomprehensible and implausible: we have been unable to use it to awaken the conscience of the world, or even of ourselves in the face of violence, lies, and hypocrisy, and often we have allowed it to soothe and anesthetize us when we should have been disquieted and aroused. Often our words have lost their salty savor and become worthless. That is why "God died" in our culture and in the language of our contemporaries; "We killed God" by draining God's name of meaning and devaluing it, by inscribing it on our battle flags, by sneaking it as an advertising gimmick into speeches that are propaganda for our own political aims. We have sullied it in pamphlets of labored "proofs" of God's existence, and in barrels of bigoted balderdash full of threadbare clichés.

The only place where the word *God* can reacquire meaning, after being forgotten, mutilated, and now scrupulously displaced, is in the story of Jesus. Even if the whole world lay in the shadow of "God's death," there is always just one place where God can be encountered alive: in Christ, in Jesus of Nazareth. Everything we have "known" and said about God can and must die—we do not know God apart from what speaks to us in Christ, through him, with him, and in him. As Bonhoeffer maintained, like Paul and Luther before him, the world has meaning only because Jesus once walked through it. The apostle Paul literally wrote: "I regard everything as loss because of the surpassing value of knowing Christ Jesus my Lord. For his sake I have suffered the loss of all things, and I regard them as rubbish, in order that I may gain Christ—I decided to know nothing among you except Jesus Christ, and him crucified."[23]

Nevertheless I cannot refrain from putting a number of critical questions to the most radical theologians of the death of God, who focus so much on Jesus's humanity that they allow all divinity of

God the Father and the divinity of Christ to "die" and dismiss them by reducing them to a cipher of humanity.[24] When perceived in this way, doesn't Jesus become in the end the object of a kind of idolatry? Doesn't he become too abstract and dead? Isn't he transformed in the end into some kind of "model of humanity," instead of the Jesus of the Gospels and Jesus Christ of the Christian tradition, faith, and piety? Why should he of all people be the sole "representative of God on earth"? If he is separated from the Father and definitively stripped of his divinity, doesn't that reduce him simply to a unique and outstanding historical figure?

Contrary to the view of humanists, however, Christian faith recognizes Jesus Christ not as a unique personality but as a unique *person*—the "person of the Son." A person—according to Thomas Aquinas and many other theologians of the Trinity—is above all a *relationship*. Jesus lives fundamentally in a relationship and by a relationship. He *is* the relationship with the Father, and at the same time he is the relationship with us and to us. That would seem to be what the Chalcedonian dogma of the "two natures" was seeking to express above all. If we regard Jesus, not with the eyes of historians (who truly have little to tell us about him), but with a theological gaze, then we will understand him only in the context of the "Trinity"—in his relationship with the Father and relationship with the Spirit, in which he is also present in us. Of course Jesus descended into the abyss of human alienation from God—thereby experiencing "the death of God" from the other side, as it were. But he did not remain "an orphan," and he also won't *leave us as orphans*.[25] This what the message of "the Resurrection" means.

Doesn't atheism itself, even more than the work of the "death of God theologians," reflect most faithfully the "emptiness of the Holy of Holies" revealed when the veil was torn, or the total abandonment by God that Jesus experienced on the cross? I have tried in a number of texts—often with reference to the mystics, and Teresa of Lisieux in particular—to deal in a similar spirit with the "atheism of pain" as mysterious participation in that Good Friday moment.

I need to make one thing clear at the outset: when I speak about atheism, I have in mind, of course, atheism as a system of thought and a specific intellectual stance. I am not speaking about *people* who simply don't share our religious faith—there are lots of people like that, and lots of reasons why they don't; there have been in the past and will be in the future, and I would never dream of passing any sweeping judgment on them. When I talk about types of atheism, I am thinking of them as "ideal types" in the sense of Max Weber: as certain intellectual models to which nothing in concrete reality corresponds "100 percent." Every atheist has their own style of atheism, just as every believer has their own style of faith. So long as they are thoughtful and sensitive individuals, and not simply repeating borrowed clichés, people's verbal statements, even when they seem uniform, usually conceal an infinite range of ideas, notions, fantasies, knowledge, and experiences, which are not evident to us (and of which they too are usually not fully aware).

Atheists' notions, feelings, and arguments are no longer by any means something Christians should or must fear. Some of the themes of "death of God theology" and "theology of the cross" have enabled a certain type of atheism (critique of religion) to become a useful ally of theology. Atheist criticism helps theology to undertake important groundwork and clear the field, nipping in the bud overprimitive and sometimes truly destructive notions about God, and overthrowing idols. *Cum grano salis*, we can say that atheist criticism can thus become a "handmaiden of contemporary theology," albeit in a somewhat different way than medieval theology regarded metaphysics as an *ancilla* (handmaiden) of theology.

Like fire, however, atheism can be a "good servant but a bad master." The postmodern philosopher Peter Sloterdijk points out, for instance, that atheism and materialism were interesting when they were a critique of religion, theology, and metaphysics but that they became embarrassing when they departed from this role and turned themselves into a quasi-metaphysical system. (In my country, we, recall "scientific atheism" being presented as a "scientific discipline" as part of Marxist-Leninist doctrine!)

So long as notions of God as an object, an entity among entities, a "being" like created beings, about which one can argue whether or not it "exists," continue to survive, then the theologian must welcome an atheism that destroys such notions, because *there really is no such God*. If someone describes God as a "supernatural being," somewhere behind the scenes, then by all means toss that notion straight into the furnace of atheist criticism. The God we believe in is not "behind reality" but is the depths of reality, its mystery.

God is "the reality of realities." We employ the metaphor of "person" for God not because we regard God as something like a created finite being. Our intention is to express two things above all. First, *it is possible to reach out to God, and God reaches out to us* (we can reach out to God in prayer, and God reaches out to us in our lives and reality in general. Second, *God is fundamentally in a relationship*. We believe in a God who lives in the communion of the Trinity—in other words, God is a Father in a relationship with the Son and through the Son and the Spirit is in a fundamental relationship with us people. Christianity asserts that God is not God without or outside of a relationship with people, and humans are not fully human without and outside of a relationship with God (and they are in a relationship with God even when they are not aware of that relationship, when they "do not believe in God," and do not call God by the same name as Christians). God has a story even with every "atheist."

If atheism wanted to be truly consistent and strip humans of their fundamental relationship with the foundation and depths of reality, as well as with the reality and mystery of their own lives and everything that radically transcends them (i.e., everything that faith denotes with the word *God*), it would end up with a "dead," totally abstract and unreal human being. The fact is (happily) that human beings without any relationship at all to the transcendental *do not exist*. It is as much a fiction as a "God behind the scenes" of reality, the world, and history.

A consistent atheism that "left God out" would in fact leave humankind out.[26]

When, in the mid-1990s, the Vatican abolished the Pontifical Council for Dialogue with Non-believers (as apparently being redundant by then), I thought it was a somewhat premature and inappropriately triumphalist gesture, most likely provoked by the unexpectedly sudden collapse of the empire of compulsory state atheism. But now it is increasingly apparent to me that insofar as contemporary theology has understood that the mental models of classical metaphysics are really no longer viable, insofar as it has taken seriously many of the atheists' justified criticisms of certain forms of religion, and insofar as Christian spirituality perceives faith as a *journey,* in the course of which crises and "dark nights" of faith can occur, classical atheism has lost the plot and had the wind taken out of its sails. I also have shifted somewhat from my study of atheism in favor of dialogue with non-Christian religions and contemporary philosophical thinking, which I feel offers livelier stimulus and better prospects. Enlightenment atheism has given way in great measure to the radical secularization of public life, which is more of a political and psychological issue. Intellectually speaking, there is nothing in that variety of liberalism of interest to theological or philosophical criticism. Likewise the current disputes between creationists and scientistic neo-Darwinists seem to me like a tragicomic dialogue of the deaf, and I regret that neither side has learnt to think philosophically. I am sorry for the biblical fundamentalists that by clinging to a superficial "literal interpretation" of biblical texts they fail to see the true depth and richness of those writings. And when, on the other hand, I think of all the things that those who want to disbelieve in creation and a Creator are required to believe, and how they have to tie themselves in knots in order to endow Chance and Natural Selection with divine characteristics and providential attributes, the "creation hypothesis" seems to me more rational, logical, and natural.

Neither the all-too-transparent God of the fundamentalist creationists who finished his work in six days, nor the divinized blind Chance that fails to inspire or concede any questions about the deeper meaning of that work, can be for me an object of my belief and veneration. I see no reason why evolutionary biology and critical scientific rationality as a whole—now that previous unfortunate disputes have been overcome long ago—should come into any kind of conflict with religious respect for the ultimate mystery of being—so long as they are able to be equally critical of themselves and recognize their own limitations, particularly in view of the fact that present-day theological hermeneutics presents the language of that mystery in the form of intelligent interpretation and does not try to provide "proofs," which would ultimately devalue the mystery and render it meaningless.

The *atheism of suffering* ("Although I'd like to, I can't believe because of the suffering in the world," the *atheism of protest and struggle with God* (from Job to Nietzsche), the *atheism* (or rather agnosticism) *of reticence* (that rejects the language of religion because of a reluctance to give any name to the ultimate mystery of life)—all can and should be treated with great respect and should be regarded not only as a "servant" but as a partner of faith and theology. But in the final analysis I can't help thinking that all the interesting types of atheism were really only interesting in the context of tension with a certain kind of faith. Atheism was not only interesting but needed and clearly necessary in its critical form as a corrective of a certain kind of religion, and it has been useful insofar (and only insofar) as that problematic kind of religion (such as religion tied to political power) is significant. But is atheism *of itself* capable not only of destroying but also building something of value?

Confronted with a weaker opponent—in the post-Enlightenment Western world at least—lonesome (and hence somewhat rogue) atheism has had to come up with a new adversary (and in doing so resembles its counterpart, religious fundamentalism), or gradually to transform itself into a pseudoreligion—often, surprisingly soon, starting to copy the failings (and sometimes even the crimes) of the kind of religion it was relentlessly battling. This was clearly the case of Jacobinism and Bolshevism. And how will these attempts by zealous protagonists of radical de-Christianization of Western society, which are now evident in many places, continue to evolve?

When today's inquisitors of political correctness decree the removal of Nativity scenes from the squares of English and American towns out of a hypocritical concern not to offend the sensibilities of Muslims and other minorities, Muslim storekeepers, who are not offended in the least by veneration of Jesus—whose virgin birth is recorded in the Koran—fortunately have the right to display them in

their store window. However, Muslims view with contempt our out-
wardly submissive and inwardly aggressive spiritual self-castration.

Where does post-Christian society's fear of the cross and other
symbols of Christian faith come from, seeing that they have truly
long ceased to be symbols of power or a threat to freedom, and
there is no way they can be? Christian fundamentalists, who are
anyway extremely adept at keeping alive this fanaticism of extremist
secularist fundamentalism, thereby lending it a semblance of legiti-
macy, tend to impute these efforts to dark conspiracies (freemasons,
and more recently—particularly in texts by "charismatics"—New
Age movements, etc.). I fear, however, that these endeavors actually
have even deeper roots than the paranoid theories of omnipresent
conspiracies imagine—namely in certain recesses of the human
heart that the liberating power of the Crucified One, whose journey
through the realms of darkness is the subject of the church's contemplation on Holy Saturday, has yet to reach.

When confronted by the rise of Nazism, Carl Jung declared
that a large part of Europe had clearly not yet been truly and profoundly Christianized, that the water of baptism must have simply
run off the surface of certain large groups when springs of ancient
barbarism could so quickly and easily gush from the depths of their
"collective unconscious."[27] And has any real change taken place since
those days in this respect? Shouldn't we have construed quite differently Pope John Paul II's call for a "new evangelization of Europe,"
which was mocked by his opponents as a romantic dream of recon-
quest and discredited by some of his supporters as a call for zealous religious agitation in the style of revivalist sects? Shouldn't we
have seen it as a call for the therapeutic power of the gospel to reach
the very heart of our culture—and its deepest recesses—by adopt-
ing a truly *new*, and possibly quieter, slower, but above all *deeper*
approach?

I reflected in one of my previous books on whether, in addition
to *creatio continua* (the continuing work of creation), we should
speak about *resurrectio continua*: an event that is victoriously and
definitively accomplished from God's perspective but that still continues from the perspective of human history in the depths of history and in human hearts. And if our task is to bring the message

of Christ's victory to every corner of the earth, shouldn't we be patiently bringing it to the wondrously locked and unilluminated recesses of our human nature and our culture, rather than engaging in noisy missionary activity in the streets?

Maybe we have yet to fully realize the amazing opportunity of today, now that Christianity is disappearing from our culture, after having been its *natural* framework in the form of "religion," that is, a matter of tradition, authority, collectiveness—as legacy handed down. Although Christianity brought many cultural and social benefits during the many centuries of its presence as a religion in European society, millions of Christians were clearly deprived of what is essential in Christian faith, namely, the experience of *metanoia*, conversion—not simply in the sense of conversion from unbelief to belief, or from one religion to another, but in the sense of life transformation, which Jesus of Nazareth called for (in the footsteps of the prophets).

We know from the lives of the saints (particularly Augustine, Francis of Assisi, Ignatius of Loyola, Teresa of Avila, and countless others) that they truly underwent such a conversion, a surprising transformation (which they themselves did not expect, in most cases, after all their Christian upbringing and in the midst of a "Christian society")—and I'm sure such an experience was not restricted to those whom the church accepted at its altar. Nevertheless, if we look carefully at our history it would seem that millions of good people who affirmed and practiced the Christian religion (in most cases undoubtedly sincerely and unhypocritically) calmly accepted it as a system of time-tested rules, rituals, and customs, and that their tranquility was never disturbed by the birth of faith as a free personal response to a personally discerned call from God.

Maybe here is the emptiness that the lures of this world can so easily manipulate. Maybe those who live in this wasteland bear festering wounds, which we will cure, not with missionary trumpets and drums in the spirit of Christian triumphalism ("We bring you the Truth available to us—join us and you will be saved"), but through the power of Christ's wounds, which we will also discover in ourselves as long as Christ's call for repentance, in the sense of transforming our life, has a profound impact on us.

Instead of being obsessively on the lookout for masked agents of dark forces artfully seeking to undermine "our good old religion," Christians should maybe try to see whether some stale forms of religion in our culture and society ought to be undermined by the "subversive power" of the gospel.

At the very end of his life, in his last book, *Heretical Essays*, Jan Patočka describes Christian faith as "*openness* to the abyss in the divine and human." He writes: "By virtue of this foundation in the abysmal deepening of the soul, Christianity remains thus far the greatest, unsurpassed *and also un-thought-through* human outreach that enabled humans to struggle against decadence."[28] Doesn't the path to "thinking through Christianity" start somewhere in the vicinity of the mysteries we have just been touching on?

5

A Dancing God

Richard Kearney reminds us that *perichoresis* (mutual "interpenetration" and interdependence of the persons of the Trinity), one of the key concepts of ancient Christian Trinitarian theology, is related to the notion of dance. He recalls ancient Christian depictions of the Trinity as wheels and humorously imagines the inner life of the Trinity as a dance in which the Father, Son, and Holy Spirit mutually give way to each other.[1]

That truly unusual vision instantly brought to my mind two associations: a dance by dervishes that I witnessed last year in Turkey at Konya during the annual festival to commemorate the Islamic mystic Rumi (Mevlana), a powerful physical evocation of God's dynamic love from the treasury of Sufi mysticism, and Nietzsche's words "I should believe only in a God who understood how to dance."[2] For Nietzsche, a dancing god was a symbol of divine lightness, freedom, and joy, in contrast to the "spirit of gravity" and "spirit of vengeance," ressentiment, and gloomy moralizing, which, according to Nietzsche, pervades the Christian faith and Christian morality above all.

Can Jesus—and the triune God shown to us through him—be a dancing God? The instinctive "no" that this thought immediately provokes in us is, however, more an indication that our imagination is fettered to the rather gloomy pictures of Christ in our churches. The apocryphal gospels—rare surviving documentary evidence of the spirituality of certain communities of early Christians—have no qualms about describing *Jesus dancing with* his disciples (and there is no reason why this image should be less authentic than many reminiscences preserved in the canonical gospels). Some explanations of depictions of the Crucified One, particularly the Byzantine ones, in which Jesus's body is curved in a strikingly dynamic pose, actually maintain that this depiction seeks to represent John's unity of the cross and resurrection, humiliation and elevation, and is also an illustration of the psalmist's words: *You turned my wailing into dancing.* Similarly, the resurrected Jesus *passing through closed doors* (as well as in the scene of the meeting with Thomas) has the lightness and freedom of the dance about him (maybe we could even say humor), which Nietzsche maybe craved for, having been disgusted by a God who was either a projection of an unacknowledged lust for vengeance or a powerless old man dying from his ineffectual "sympathy with people."

It is certainly not our intention here to "chisel God" into an appearance that might possibly appeal to Nietzsche and his followers. We want to understand why the arrival of the Resurrected One aroused in Thomas that ecstatic state of joy in which he blurted out: "My Lord and my God!"—and also, of course, to ask in all humility whether and how *we* might share in that paschal joy.

After all, aren't this joy and this freedom precisely the "cornerstone" of Christian faith, which all pious (and impious), gloomy, dull, cheerless, self-absorbed people who succumb to the "spirit of gravity" are bound to collide with? If we want to get onto the dance floor of Easter freedom, don't we need precisely that "childlike spirit" that Jesus spoke of when he promised the Kingdom of God to those who have the humility and courage to be "born again" and become children once more?[3] (And hadn't Nietzsche experienced something of that mystery when he had his Zarathustra prophesy in the chapter "The Three Metamorphoses" that the ascetic bearer of burdens must become not only the lion of free will and sovereign strength but also, in the end, a child, free even from itself?)[4]

What would prevent *us* from stepping into the light of that Easter freedom in place of Thomas the apostle, and joyfully repeating his declaration? Where is our "locked door" with which we defend ourselves from the mystery of the Resurrection? Maybe we are not free of questions, whose ponderous skepticism (inherited from the materialism of previous centuries and its too-narrow understanding of reality) we often project onto Thomas's doubts: What is the Resurrection "really" about?

In his profound and original "summa teologica,"[5] the Polish theologian Tomasz Weclawski makes an important comment: Those who ask questions such as "What really happened to Jesus's body, lying in the tomb?" or "What (or whom) did those who said they saw Jesus risen from the dead actually see?" thereby reveal that they are under a profound misapprehension, because these very questions show that those who ask them believe they *already know* what "resurrection" is and are simply seeking confirmation whether and to what extent what they themselves associate with the word corresponds to what is said here about Jesus, and whether the witnesses to those events in fact saw and experienced what, according to them, they were supposed and permitted to see and experience.

But if we really think theologically, we know that we do not know the meaning of the metaphor "resurrection," and likewise—as St. Thomas Aquinas was always stressing—we do not know who God "really" is (what "God's self" is like). God's self and the Resurrection are radical mysteries that are beyond the limits of our apprehension, our language, our logic, and our imagination; we do not have the power to take possession of them and dispose of them as we would an item of knowledge and possession—we can relate to them only through faith and hope, and listen to the extent that these mysteries themselves (perhaps) speak to us. The most we know is that we are fundamentally dependent on these mysteries and that it would be extremely foolish (albeit humanly understandable) were we to turn our backs on them indifferently because they are "shrouded in a mist."

To return to Weclawski:

God is invisible to us, just as the future is invisible. The future awaits us and keeps arriving, but so long as it remains the future it cannot be observed. The future will only show itself when it becomes our present—and, moreover, only within us and our history. God also becomes visible when God becomes the human present, but at that moment he is visible not as

God, but as a human being and as a human story—in the life, death, and resurrection of Jesus Christ and everything that appertains to God. And yet in Jesus God also remains invisible—as God. And we can add: like the future inasmuch as it remains the future. But there the analogy ends: although God is our future, the future isn't our God. God therefore does not cease to be invisible qua God, when the future that is open in Jesus becomes a visible present.[6]

God (as God is "in God's self" and "of God's self") will always remain a mystery accessible only to faith and hope, and thus also exposed to doubt. We have already seen that sentences about the "death of God" need not offend even Christians of a traditional faith (such as I am also) provided that they read it as a diagnosis of the world and its capacity to be open to that Mystery; the point is that—provided they are theological statements and not empty rhetoric—they are not statements about "God as such," because a theologian knows that ultimately "God as such" defies all human statements ("from below").

The Resurrection equally remains a mystery of the future, which is beyond our experience, one to which we can only relate now through faith and hope without the "safety rope" of rational proof, and which we cannot truly "understand" and experience until we ourselves have crossed the threshold of death. Perhaps all we do know is what Christ's resurrection *is not*, or to put it another way, what scripture clearly does not mean by that word. It does not mean—and unfortunately this must be repeated over and over again!—either "reanimation" or "resuscitation" of a corpse and its mere return to this world, subject to time, space, and death ("Christ, being raised from the dead, will never die again; death no longer has dominion over him," St. Paul explicitly states),[7] but it does not seek to be simply a symbolic transcription of the idea that Jesus's ideas or "Jesus's cause" goes marching on—it is necessary to take seriously the gospel accounts that the witness encountered a person, not an ideology.

While I have no wish to detract from Weclawski's compelling reading of the invisibility of God and the future, I must nonetheless point to experiences that seem to fall like "sparks of the future" (divine sparks) into the human present; although these do not enable us to "see" the future (and God) and "take control of them," they do rouse us from sticking lazily to what has been achieved and known in the past and present. Such experiences would also seem to include Thomas's encounter with the Resurrected One; that light of Jesus's *transformed* wounds enabled him for a moment to see through the man to God, through the present to the future, through the visible to the Invisible.

But let us not dance too quickly and impetuously into the light of Thomas's confession and that entire gospel scene!

"If you meet Christ, kill him!" Such a statement from the lips of a Catholic priest certainly sounds somewhat unusual, to put it mildly—as it did to me when I first heard it. But it's always wise not to rush to judgment. I expect that even someone who has never studied Wittgenstein's philosophy of language will accept his principle that we reveal the real meaning of each sentence not in the sentence itself but in the context in which it was spoken or written.

This was the context: it was said to me by one of the greatest practical and theoretical authorities on the mysticism and meditation of East and West among twentieth-century Christians, the Jesuit and Zen master Fr. Enomyia Lassalle, who worked for decades in Japan. It was during a *dokusan*—a private conversation, whereby a novice of Zen meditation may interrupt his silence once a day to put specific questions to his master. When I admitted to repeating the name of Jesus to help me focus during meditation, he told me it was "heretical Zen." True Zen—if people, whether Buddhists, Christians, Jews, or atheists, want to practice it authentically, according to the teaching of ancient masters—aims at the total emptying of the mind of all notions, images, words, and names—even the greatest ones. (Didn't we touch on the same mystery of the dialectic of emptiness and fullness when meditating on the mystery of Christ's pierced heart, the empty Holy of Holy of the Jerusalem temple, the torn curtain, "the death of God," and the withdrawal of God in the mysticism of the Kabbalah, in the apophatic tradition, in Luther's theology of the cross, in "death of God theology," and in the postmodern interpreters of secularism as the self-emptying of God?) Buddhist masters warned against the "pious notions" of their Buddhist novices: "If you meet the Buddha, kill him!" So why shouldn't a Christian Zen master say in the same sense to his Christian novice, "If you meet Christ, kill him!"?

These words, which undoubtedly sound blasphemous to many Christians, were explained to me later by another teacher of meditation (in a somewhat less koan-like manner) as follows. In contemplation we do not place God or God's only-begotten Son "before us" as the object of meditation; rather, we try to experience what it means—in the words of St. Paul—"to be in Christ" and feel that *it is no longer I who live, but it is Christ who lives in me.*[8]

It is in fact just another way to express the ideas of the apostle Paul, who stressed that he did not want to know *Jesus according to the flesh*, "physically" (from the outside), but "*according to the spirit*," in a spiritual inward way. Here Paul was certainly defending his own approach to Christ's mystery: unlike the other apostles he did not know "the historical Jesus" (and quite frankly in his theology about Jesus—with the exception of the Easter events—he expressed very little interest in his life story). What affected and transformed him was above all the shocking vision of the Crucified One that he experienced on the road to Damascus, as well as the testimony of the disciples (including the martyrdom of Stephen that preceded Paul's conversion) and his meditation in the Arabian deserts, where the fundamentals of his theology would seem to have matured.

Likewise, the deeper meaning of the apostle Thomas's meeting with the Risen One that we reflect on in this book needs to be looked for in the context of the gospel narrative: it takes place in the "in-between" time between Easter and the Ascension, at the time of preparation for when Christ's followers will no longer see, know, and touch him as "Christ according to the flesh," but rather will know him in *Spirit*. To know Christ "according to the spirit" and dwell in him means "to have the spirit of Christ,"[9] and more (here the strains of mysticism in Paul's and John's sources meet): to be united by the Spirit, the living bond of unity between Father and Son, mutually united, united with Christ and thereby drawn into the "heart of the Trinity."

That is the other side of Easter, the counterpart to the Good Friday and Easter Saturday "emptying" (*kenosis*), and these two sides belong to each other like breathing out and breathing in, like the systole and diastole (to use the favorite expression of the staunch atheist Ludwig Feuerbach in a somewhat contrary sense to the one he used regarding the relationship of man and God).[10]

The journey on which Thomas encounters Christ is not just a scene of meeting but also a journey of leave-taking, as Jesus is "going to his Father."[11] But his departure fulfills the hour whose imminent arrival was prophesied by Jesus to the Samaritan woman at the well, when God's true worshippers will worship God, not here or there, but *in Spirit and truth*.[12] If he hadn't left us, we could not have been given the Spirit.[13]

"The God who is with us is the God who forsakes us," Pastor Bonhoeffer wrote in prison in the period before his execution, and he drew the following conclusion: "God would have us know that we must live as men who manage our lives without him."[14]

We must do without God as external support. With a God who is only *external* (Christ according to the flesh) we would never achieve the freedom and joy of God's dancing sons and daughters. We would be more like caricatures of that "spirit of childhood" that Christ calls for. We would remain infantile, immature, clumsy, and incapable of responsibility. If ever you are offered an external Christ "according to the flesh"—and, sadly, be prepared to come across such a concept of Christ in the pulpits of our churches and in today's religious marketplace—reject such an image: "Kill it!" Instead search with the apostle for "Christ according to the Spirit," in whom you can dwell and mature.

In Christ, as he passes through the cross to the Father, God leaves us in order to give us a space of freedom and responsibility— the space of the Spirit, in which we can discover Christ anew, no longer on the surface but in depth. Not in a private self-contained chamber of devotion (which would truly be a perverse interpretation of the inwardness of the Spirit), but in the depth of the reality in which we are placed and of which we are part. Let us not forget that one of the rarest prophetic gifts of the Spirit is the art of "reading the signs of the times": understanding today as a challenge from God.

The gospel scene with Thomas ends with a blessing of those *who do not see and yet have come to believe.* Yes, it is a journey to the "invisible" yet present Christ, a journey of discovery, disclosing his new and different presence, no longer via the senses, or the nonsense of meaningless pious clichés, but through faith, hope, and love. It is a journey that we may hope will end, after all our often-convoluted adventures, in ecstatic participation in the divine ring dance, in the embrace of the Trinity.

6

Worshipping the Lamb

It is said that on the night before the Battle of the Milvian Bridge the emperor Constantine saw the sign of the cross in a vision and heard the words: "In this sign you shall conquer!" So he had crosses fixed to the banners of his troops and slaughtered his enemies. Out of gratitude he legitimized the previously persecuted church and in addition gave it privileges, following which Christianity became the state religion of the Roman Empire.

I can't help wondering how the history of Christianity, Europe, and the world would have turned out if Emperor Constantine had interpreted the rare revelation he received more intelligently.

Maybe without Constantine's gifts the church might not have developed its cultural potential to such an extent, maybe if Christianity had not enjoyed such scope in the limelight of the empire in which the sun never set it might not have been able to permeate society with its therapeutic power, and it might not have been able to create educational and social institutions, or bring a rich harvest of the beneficial fruits of its influence for a thousand years. Maybe. But maybe in that imperial version of Christianity something fundamental was forgotten and not developed. In fact, it was betrayed and distorted.

To give thought to what was forgotten is not a mere game of fantasy on the shaky premise of "What if?," which history does not permit, as we know. It is looking for a treasure that Christians found in the field of history but—as scripture advises them—carefully buried again. And they didn't always have an opportunity "to buy the field" afterward. Some of them, disgusted by Roman official Christianity, carried the treasure of what was forgotten in an exodus of protest—what a historical irony—back into the Egyptian desert, where they established the first monasteries, hotbeds of "alternative Christianity." In all events, for us today, when the last vestiges of Constantine's Christianity are on the point of collapse in the West (I don't mean the church's position of power—that collapsed through the Enlightenment—but Christianity as the *natural* framework of our civilization), the search for what remained undeveloped under the golden sands of officialdom and public favor could be not only of interest but actually vitally important. It could help us build a house of faith this time truly on rock, bare rock, and not on the shining but treacherous sands of protection by the powerful.

After "the death of God" in public space, language, and culture, Christ comes to us today and shows us his wounds. He points to the cross that was intended to serve as a mirror for "emperors," in which they would have the rare chance to see their nakedness, but that was never intended for emperors to use to adorn their fictive "new clothes"—their armor, weapons, and battle standards— like a magic amulet.

Christianity belongs in politics, but as a critical opponent of power, fulfilling the important but thankless and dangerous role of the prophets: divesting power of the sacred aura that it loves to don, and showing—as Nathan did to David—that kings are also only people and should not act like gods. The cross belongs in "public space," not as an august monument of victory, but above all as a reminder of those who paid dearly for every victory of power.

Christ comes to us and does not conceal his wounds but displays them in order to give us the courage to remove our armor, our masks, and our makeup and look not only at the wounds and scars that we conceal beneath them from others and often from ourselves but also at the wounds we have inflicted on others.

Albert Speer, Hitler's chief architect and later minister of armaments and war production, explained to his daughter after the war: "You must realize that at the age of 32, in my capacity as an architect, I had the most splendid assignments of which I could dream. Hitler said to your mother one day that her husband could design buildings the like of which had not been seen for 2000 years. One would have had to be morally very stoical to reject the proposal. But I was not at all like that." Speer added that he wanted to be an architect above all, and so out of fear of exposing something that might divert him from his path, *he closed his eyes*.[1] I live and work alongside lots of people who, in the same spirit and for the same reason—and for a much smaller mess of pottage—sold their souls to the second totalitarian regime of the twentieth century.

Encountering Christ is dangerous, because through his wounds he removes our dark glasses, *opens our eyes*, and leads us away from those paths that we so often readily take "with eyes closed."

Readers will not find in this book instructions for how to heal the wounds of our world, and possibly they don't even seek them. I have always been highly distrustful of all recipes for salvation. If my reflections seek to be of some assistance, then it is in urging "nonindifference" and the courage to see. After all, everyone must decide for themselves whether, how, to what extent, and where specifically they want and can get involved in efforts to heal human wounds—assuming, of course, that they are capable of perceiving them.

I admit that at certain moments in India, Myanmar, or Egypt (in the awful cemetery in the center of Cairo, where possibly tens of thousands of poor people literally live in tombs!) I was tempted not to see, to close my eyes and heart and get away from there as fast as possible. A Jesuit who had worked for decades in India told me that after his arrival in Calcutta he was tempted for a long time by two immature, escapist reactions in turn: a childish reaction—closing his eyes and hiding his face in any substitute for his mother's skirts before fleeing the place, and the adolescent reaction of the enraged revolutionary: to reach for weapons and forcefully annihilate the unjust social conditions along with those who were responsible for and prospered from them! It was only through dint of long hours, nay years, of meditation that he gained the strength to persevere and overcome the seduction of impatience and see through the illusions of quick paths to salvation.

J. B. Metz speaks of the need for a "mysticism of open eyes," which is clearly a polemical reference to Oriental meditation with closed eyes. Another Christian author takes even more stringent issue with Buddhism: whereas Buddhism teaches how to escape suffering by "freeing oneself from *attachment*" and by the extinction of the ego, Christianity, on the contrary, calls on us to bind our ego to others and nail it to the cross of solidarity until "blood and water" flows from our own heart, to *see* the wounds of the world and allow ourselves to be wounded by them, to overcome selfishness, not by ascetic techniques and contemplation, but by allowing prayer to give rise to actions of practical love and concrete assistance to our neighbors. I remember that I was somewhat cured of the Western fascination with Far Eastern spirituality when, in India, I repeatedly came across Hindu devotees complaining about the charitable activities of the Missionaries of Charity founded by Mother Teresa. They maintained that these Christians simply prevented the poor from suffering for the sins of their past lives and being rewarded by a better fate in their next rebirth.

I do not intend at this point to join Christians' debates with yogis and Buddhists. I have debated with Buddhist monks (i.e., not with people in the West who often flirt with Buddhism without commitment and sometimes rather comically), and I have spent time in Japanese monasteries—albeit not years, but long enough to be cautious about making sweeping judgments. It seems to me that those who too easily equate the paths of Far Eastern and Christian mysticism, as well as those who dramatically counterpose them, are equally guilty of oversimplification. It is possible to find enough examples and arguments for both attitudes in the many different schools that exist in those rich and vast spiritual worlds.

To return to what I was told by that Jesuit missionary, I would add that meditation not only nourishes the courage to persevere but also gives rise to actions that can be truly therapeutic—unlike escape or revolution. Let us recall the work of two people of prayer and meditation whose tireless activity qualitatively changed the face and spirit of India to a certain extent—although of course it did not cure all its social and political problems. I refer to Mahatma Gandhi and Mother Teresa of Calcutta!

Hans Urs von Balthasar wrote a remarkable sentence: "Whoever does not come to know the face of God in contemplation will not recognize it in action, even when it reveals itself to him in the face of the oppressed and humiliated."

There is one fundamental characteristic of actions that grow out of contemplation, and that is *nonviolence*. By consistently refusing "to play with cards dealt by evil," they contribute a truly new quality to our world.

"The war on terrorism" declared by President Bush after September 11, 2001, became unwinnable as soon as the president went along with Al Qaeda's apocalyptic rhetoric: the Great Satan, the Evil Empire; us good, them evil. . . .

Even if the American president did not mean it "literally," even if it was simply rhetoric, whose aim is naturally to mobilize and unite the nation (for a while, at least), it was nevertheless an extremely dangerous enterprise. Even in a "secular epoch" and a secular society, religious expressions and symbols have an enormous power (often unrecognized and naively underestimated by "secular people"). When the power of religious symbols is combined with the power of weapons, such an unholy alliance—like all such marriages of religion and politics—will sooner or later beget chimeras and monsters.[2]

Satan cannot be destroyed by bombs. He can only be eradicated. I can eradicate him from the world only if I start with my own world, my own heart and "unconscious"—chiefly by discovering him as the *shadow* of my own ego, as an unacknowledged part, which we enjoy projecting into the world—onto "others." Monsters and nightmares (which so readily implant themselves in relationships and penetrate even the political sphere from the infernos of our unconscious) can be overcome, Richard Kearney suggests, only if we find the courage to look at them in the face.[3] At that moment, we discover they are not so unlike ourselves as we imagined when, on account of our fear and hatred (which anyway most frequently spawned them or summoned them from hell), we perceived them as "faceless beings."

We banish demons by naming them. So long as we already know their real names they can have no power over us. God cannot be banished, declares the somewhat triumphalist title of a book by Luděk Pachman.

Another reason God cannot be banished is that God doesn't have such a name (as we well know from the scene when God is presented to Moses in the burning bush).[4] Our attempts to "define God" (i.e., delimit God), to depict God, or to think up some names or formulas that we could use to summon God to our service and political interests whenever we fancied, are condemned in the Bible as a mortal sin against faith, as magic and idolatry.

Since our God has no name, God can neither be summoned at human whim nor banished. This Nameless One remains with us also in an anonymous form—even where we don't recognize, acknowledge, or invoke God. God also remains with us *nonvocatus*—"invoked or not invoked," as the inscription on the tomb of Carl Gustav Jung declares.

The gods who, in the text from Nietzsche's *Zarathustra* referred to earlier, so ridiculed the Jewish God's claim to uniqueness, did so rather prematurely. The God of the Jews also survived those gods because of God's closely guarded anonymity.

Christian faith says that the only thing that can penetrate the cloud of God's hiddenness and break the seals on the gates of silence of God's inaccessible anonymity is the name (i.e., personality, humanity) of God's only-begotten Son. We can approach God and invite God into our lives and world if we address God in the name of God's Son, if we ask God *in the name* of God's Son, the gospel says.[5]

In our own day, even among Christians in the West, the "pearl of Orthodoxy," the so-called Jesus Prayer, or simply the repetition of Jesus's name, is gaining popularity again, and it is one that I also frequently recite.[6] But only now do I begin to perceive it in a broader context: in a world of violence from which God seems absent, in which we have to do without God as an external support, as Pastor Bonhoeffer taught us from his death cell, we cannot do without "the name of Jesus"—without constant reminiscence (*anamnesis*) of Jesus and his path.

This *anamnesis*, as Jesus says in John's Gospel, is the sending of the Holy Spirit—who "will teach you everything, and remind you of all that I have said to you."[7] It is not simply a matter of alerting our somnolent attention, as when a note in our diary reminds us of a task we haven't done, but a deeper understanding of what emerges from "memory." For Augustine and many Christian thinkers influenced by Plato, memory is where the soul encounters God with greatest intensity: the depths—probably what the Bible (and Pascal) call "the heart" and what depth psychology calls "the unconscious" or *das Selbst* (self).

When we continually remember Christ (as in the celebration of the Eucharist—the remembrance of his death), this also gives us the strength to be watchful, the strength to refuse soothing drugs of various kinds (Marx would undoubtedly be amazed at the kind of "opiates of the people" a religionless world is capable of offering!), along with all kinds of intoxicating and seductive means of anaesthetizing our conscience.

One of the outstanding fathers of ancient Christianity, Clement of Alexandria, compared the way that the Christian is bonded to the cross of Christ with the situation of the hero of Homeric epics Odysseus, who first filled his companions' ears with wax and then lashed himself to the mast of his ship in order to hear without danger the enticing song of the Sirens, which had lured all previous ships to places where they would shipwreck: "Sail past the song; it works death. Exert your will only, and you have overcome ruin; bound to the wood of the cross, thou shalt be freed from destruction: the word of God will be thy pilot, and the Holy Spirit will bring thee to anchor in the haven of heaven. Then shalt thou see my God, and be initiated into the sacred mysteries, and come to the fruition of those things which are laid up in heaven reserved for me, which 'ear hath not heard, nor have they entered into the heart of any.'"[8] Those who cleave to Christ and the mast of his cross are in Paul's words "crucified to the world and to him."[9] Then they can hear all those voices of the world without fear of being confused and diverted from their path, says that teacher of Christian wisdom.

⌒ Let this be a moment to introduce a comment about my ongoing decades-long dialogue with my first philosophical love— Nietzsche—in my thinking, my faith, and my works. "It is typical of Nietzsche that when he errs he also says something profound," commented one of his theological commentators. I would not make so bold as to judge where "Nietzsche erred" and where he maybe just provocatively counterbalanced our errors, or our one-sidedness with an opposite extreme. Nietzsche admits that he always has "two opinions about everything." So when he sees that we are excessively fascinated by the light of day, he urgently reminds us in a dramatic fashion that there also exists the depth of night. When our speech is too sweet, he speaks to us in a voice full of salt, wormwood, and vinegar. When he detects in our sentimental piety a hidden impiety, he demonstrates his capacity to speak with God and about God as the "most pious of the godless," who would not reject our Savior—on condition that we ourselves appeared more redeemed.

I know that for many of those who have read Nietzsche's refusal to be "bound to Christ" and the *mast of the cross,* his writing became a Siren that lured them to a tragic shipwreck. Nevertheless, I am convinced that those who have accepted Christ "without distance" and who, like Odysseus, do not have their ears blocked with wax, would greatly benefit from listening carefully to Nietzsche.

⌒ Mere mechanical repetition is not a way of remembering Jesus's name. That would be to "take his name in vain" and give into magic; one cannot "lash oneself to the mast of the cross," or "crucify the flesh with its passions and desires,"[10] simply by pious and comforting feelings. "All sufferers can find comfort in the solidarity of the Crucified," writes Miroslav Volf, "but only those who struggle against evil by following the example of the Crucified will discover him at their side. To claim the comfort of the Crucified by rejecting his way is to advocate not only cheap grace but a deceitful ideology."[11]

Those who are crucified to the world by the memory of Christ's wounds cherish within themselves "Christ's mind." They do not seek to know Christ "according to the flesh" (and will never permit God's name and Christ's name to be exteriorized in the war rhetoric of power and violence). They confess "Christ according to the spirit" and live and struggle in his spirit. They enter again and again the field of a battle that can never be entirely "won" in this world but must be undertaken again and again. They must have the courage to be brought to their knees, to be *stigmatized*, and even to enter the darkness of Christ's feeling of abandonment—in the hope that not even then, or at any other time, can they, through any fault of their own, fall out of the embrace of the arms outstretched on the cross.

Those who have been brought to their knees in this world through violence and malice and have not allowed themselves to be drawn into the game of violence and hatred, those who have "washed their robes. . . in the blood of the Lamb," who "have come out of the great ordeal," are prophesied by Revelation to have a part in the liturgy in which all will finally fall upon their knees before the Lamb and sing a new song: "You are worthy to take the scroll and to open its seals, for you were slaughtered and by your blood you ransomed for God saints from every tribe and language and people and nation."[12]

Yes, there are seals that only stigmatized hands can break.

Stigmata and Forgiveness

The late archbishop of Prague, Cardinal Tomášek, who, I believe, was an eyewitness to the attempted assassination of John Paul II on St. Peter's Square, once told me about his conversation with the wounded pope when he visited him in his hospital in Rome about ten days after the attack. In reply to the customary question about how he was, the pope, lying in bed, indicated with his eyes his bandaged hands attached to instruments, and his bandaged stomach, and said with a smile: "Well, I'm stigmatized!"

In the following years those words flashed through my mind three more times: when I saw the pope ritually opening the Holy Door on the threshold of the new millennium; when I watched the tragic moments of September 11, 2001; and finally, when I saw a short video of the pope's visit to the cell of the would-be assassin.

I found it moving that the door to the new millennium should be opened by this particular pope, who opened it with stigmatized hands. Wasn't the attempt on the pope's life some kind of prophetic sign? By bearing on his own body a wound, which in the course of less than a quarter of a century would prove to be the most menacing wound of the coming era—the violence of terrorist attacks—didn't the pope fulfill a warning role similar to that demanded by the Lord from the Old Testament prophets, namely, symbolically to foretoken through their fate and behavior what would soon befall all people?

And didn't that same pope answer the question of how to truly heal those wounds when many years later he raised from the floor and embraced the man who had so painfully imperiled his life? (Perhaps many others experienced what I did when they watched that brief video, which was so reminiscent of Rembrandt's painting of the Return of the Prodigal Son, namely, a longing to be there for at least a moment, but also gratitude that the cameras were immediately switched off and the media were unable to turn that Rembrandtesque scene into sentimental kitsch.)

No, don't twist my words: I don't believe that terrorism would have vanished from the world if President Bush had gone to embrace Osama bin Laden (or the Satan he found to replace him, Saddam Hussein). I don't think that the pope's actions are universally applicable, or that there is only one recipe for curing the world's ills. I know that there are moments when one must use armed force to defend oneself and others.

But at least one thing applies universally: we must not allow violence and hatred to triumph by drawing us onto their field of play where they would envenom us with their poisonous hatred, thereby clouding our brains and hearts and rendering us incapable of taking sensible and responsible decisions, forcing us to play by their evil rules, poisoning our language and tainting our lips with words that kill, with which they themselves inflame the spirit of vengeance and trigger a spiral of revenge, thus keeping the flame of permanent war alive in the world. Only when we refuse to capitulate in this way to evil and do not become a part of it will the human family perhaps walk without fear of mutual destruction along the path of the third millennium of the Christian era, the door to which was opened by a courageous pope with stigmatized hands.

For the past twenty years a large, somewhat expressionistic painting has hung on the wall in front of my desk in Prague. On it the resurrected Christ shows the marks of nails on his enormous hands, while the wound in his side shines through the fabric of his robe. And here, too, in the hermitage, I have before my eyes a reproduction of a painting with a similar theme; and the Eucharist on the altar—does this not also point to the same mystery of Bread broken for hungry pilgrims?

When the resurrected Jesus, transformed by death, first came to the circle of his disciples (it is written that Thomas was not with them that time), when he first showed them his wounds as a kind of proof of his identity, he came to bring them a great gift: the spirit of forgiveness.

"The Johannine Pentecost," as some describe this scene in John's Gospel, in which the spirit is imparted, offers, not the "gift of tongues," as in the analogous scene in the Acts of the Apostles, but the language of forgiveness. But this is also above all an instrument for understanding and reaching agreement with people who would otherwise remain strangers to us, or even enemies.

Maybe what shocked the disciples most about the Resurrected One was not the discovery that the person they took to be dead was alive—there are several such scenes in the Bible, and they had only recently witnessed the raising of Lazarus from the tomb. Maybe what was truly radically new about the arrival of the Messiah from the darkness of torment at the hands of their enemies was above all the fact that *he did not come as an avenger but as the bringer of forgiveness*—who urges and authorizes forgiveness.[1]

One of the last parables Jesus told his disciples is maybe crucial as a riddle about what will come after his death. It is the parable of the wicked tenants.[2]

A man goes away on a journey (as God—or some figure symbolizing God—does in Jesus's parables with remarkable frequency) and sends one servant after another to the duplicitous tenants of his vineyards—and finally his own Son. But blinded by their lust for profit, and foolishly thinking that by murdering the heir they will inherit the master's property, they kill him. What will the vineyard owner do with those tenants?

The fairly logical and understandably anticipated answer, namely, that he will severely punish them, is attributed by two of the evangelists to Jesus. But one evangelist, Matthew, places the answer in the mouths of the disciples.[3] Jesus does not directly answer the question.

Not until the Resurrection do the disciples receive the shocking answer, the unexpected solution to the riddle of the parable, and the surprising outcome of the Easter mystery: God does not reap vengeance. Jesus brings peace, the Spirit, and forgiveness. His pierced palm is raised against the flames of vengeance and violence and says: Stop!

If the disciples hadn't scattered, if they had had the courage to stay beneath the cross like the women and John, they would have already heard from the cross a clear indication of the story's end: Father, forgive them, for they know not what they do.

Jesus is not speaking at this point like a naive do-gooder unaware of the black malice of those who very deliberately and single-mindedly achieved his crucifixion. They knew what they wanted—and yet they failed to grasp the ultimate significance of what they were doing.

Jesus places their action into a context that is not visible to eyes blinded by malice. It is visible to the one who is above them, in that Johannine paradox of being exalted and humiliated. Only from the painful overview from the cross, and only from the perspective from which the Son's sacrifice is viewed by the Father, who as we already know, will shortly seem even to the Son himself infinitely distant, is it possible to glimpse the real meaning of the paschal drama. The actors of the Crucifixion are unwitting accomplices in something they cannot understand—an event that halts the mechanism of vengeance and violence through the power of forgiveness.[4]

Jesus's enemies and murderers thus add wood to a fire that will no longer burn and destroy but will instead give light in which it will be possible to find a path out of hatred. The hands that the "wicked tenants" nailed to the cross will not be avenged as those who listened to Jesus's riddle expected. Those pierced hands on the cross will bring the shocking message of the vineyard owner. Instead of the God who has gone on a journey, the heir returns and says: Stop, that's enough! There are already enough unhealed sins in the world that call out for vengeance and for more and more violence. And so I tell you something that no human ears have heard before in this world, which has not before occurred to the human mind, darkened for so long by the longing for vengeance. I urgently call on you to undertake the work of healing and forgiveness: *If you forgive the sins of any, they are forgiven them; if you retain the sins of any, they are retained.* Didn't you see on the cross what unforgiven sins and unhealed malice can lead to, violence that is not halted by the power of the one who accepts the wound but does not pass it on?

Such words break down the gates of hell.

For forty days Jesus showed his wounds and taught his disciples the art of not repaying evil with evil. And then, on the day of the Ascension, he mysteriously disappeared to "the one who went on a journey." Now he too leaves history as free space in which we are to show what we learned from him. Now we are the heirs, who are in charge of the vineyard.

Looking back over the history of Christianity, we have to admit that we have often behaved less like the Son and more like the wicked tenants of the vineyard, who stoned, beat, and killed the prophets that were sent to them. For that very reason, the "millennial pope," John Paul II, made such a point of healing the wounds of the past. It is precisely why he courageously opened the dark pages of church history to the world's gaze and finally, at the beginning of Lent in the Holy Year, stood publicly before the cross and asked God and people to forgive the church all the crimes that it had committed and that it now admitted—for we too feel bound to forgive again and again all those who have done us wrong.

There is some hope in the fact that the story of history continues. There is some hope in the fact that humankind has not destroyed itself yet, even though it has more effective, rapid, and available means of doing so than ever before. There is some encouragement in the fact that the door to the new millennium was opened by a man with stigmatized hands, and that he asked us to enter it in the spirit of forgiveness—for only then can we cross the threshold of hope.

Knocking on the Wall

"Two prisoners whose cells adjoin communicate with each other by knocking on the wall. The wall is the thing which separates them but is also their means of communication. It is the same with us and God. Every separation is a link," wrote Simone Weil.[1]

Isn't that also true of our wounds, the ones we find in our lives and hearts, the wounds of people we meet, and the wounds we don't want to know about? Doesn't each of those wounds—as we saw in the different ways Pilate and Thomas viewed Christ's wounds—conceal a possibility both of separation and of connection in relation to God, or—as others call God—to the meaning of life? Isn't the experience of being wounded something *that undermines meaning* (and trust in meaningfulness), that often seems meaningless and absurd—but also something that may become *the path to a deeper understanding of meaning*, and not just of the meaning of pain that is suffered or shared?

When we talk here of wounds, we don't have in mind *only* physical pain, even though various injuries, illnesses, and congenital physical deformations can be such wounds and often are. We are not talking *only* about poverty, violence, and social injustice, even though these grievous abominations—that often "cry to heaven," biblically speaking—are naturally among the matters that we must not lose sight of. We are not talking *only* about fractures and tragically neglected "cancers" in the field of the most intimate human relationships, particularly in marriages and families, even though these are wounds that destroy so many people nowadays and that leave so many lasting unhealed scars that we never do enough to prevent and cure these "diseases of civilization." We are not talking only about the many kinds of distress suffered by so many people around us that they cannot be talked about simply as individual or private phenomena but must be seen as *wounds of the times* related to our "social sins"—such as feelings of abandonment, alienation, depression, loneliness amid city crowds, bitter grief amid the amusement parks of mass entertainment, or unfulfilled yearning for love, intimacy, and tenderness amid the din of pop songs that toss the word *love* around in every verse. I have in mind that and much more.

What I have in mind are "wounds to faith"—by which I mean much more than "religious difficulties" or problems that people with a religious faith have with the church (although these also must be included in the list of sufferings). *Because every real wound is also and in particular a wound to faith* and as such can leave scars that take the longest to heal (being often unacknowledged and untreated). In fact every real wound undermines one's (mostly implicit and unconscious) confidence that the world and life have meaning, which to a certain extent gives all of us the strength to live and survive. This faith, this trust in meaning, is what we all live on, even if we don't use religious words to describe and address that meaning. It is the primal trust that to a certain (and very different) extent we truly all share—and insofar as we share it we are healthy, that is, at ease with ourselves, and reconciled with the world and our lot in life. If there is something in people that is the "natural basis of religion" (still far removed from all its institutional, doctrinal, and ritual forms), then it is precisely this "yes" to oneself and the universe, which we affirm unconsciously with our every meaningful thought and action. The greatest pain of our woundedness is that it deflects us from that experience of meaning, that it makes us question it ("Why? Why me of all people? Why him, and not someone else?")—and the greatest danger of wounds is that they can irretrievably undermine our primal trust.

But this very question aroused in us by pain is also an opportunity for us to seek and find that meaning—to now make what we previously experienced unconsciously and implicitly the subject of our thinking and a matter of the heart. In their night of pain (and generally toward the end rather than at the beginning—in the "hour before dawn") many people have rediscovered that meaning for themselves and profoundly experienced it.

In that sense, pain is a wall that separates us from meaning (or from God, as some people call meaning) but also connects us— so long as we do not remain sitting impassively in front of it but "knock on it," and above all listen for the knocking from the other side. But it is important for us to properly understand the sign language used in such communication.

Maybe "religious education" (which a young Czech theologian and teacher has aptly termed "education in nonindifference")[2] should focus less on acquiring background knowledge of the Bible and more on trying to learn this language of symbols, without which, at a time of life trials, we can become desperately isolated prisoners.

We are talking here about our own scars, the wounds of our neighbors, and "the wounds of the world." If we now wish to reflect on them from the point of view of faith, then they really all do come to the same thing—they are all *Christ's wounds* insofar as we believe in the mystery of the Incarnation—and they are *our wounds* insofar as we realize that we cannot point to the wounds of others without showing solidarity with the wounded, without those wounds affecting us and wounding our conscience, unsettling us, and rousing us from indifference. We cannot bring something to God that is not *God's and ours at the same time*; for God (and for us insofar as we are in God), only "hell" is truly external.

Every year, the blessed summer months here in the hermitage are above all a happy time of prayer (and I also experience writing these texts as a form of prayer)—prayers of praise and gratitude, and also intercessory prayers.

What is intercessory prayer, and what is the point of it? Is it informing God of people's needs? That would be stupid. Is it sending the troubles of others and the pain of the world somewhere into the beyond with the label "Sort this out, God"? This would be passing the buck on the basis of self-deception, magic, and superstition, in other words, precisely what those who know nothing about the real spirit and sense of Christian prayer imagine intercessory prayer to be. I refer to atheists who mock it, and (alas) some believers who "practice" it in precisely this way and recommend it.

Intercessory prayer is a conversation with God about the suffering of others, which I experience as my own suffering. In this conversation—confronted with the word of the gospel, in quiet detachment from my own superficial emotions, wishes, and ideas—I learn, in the spirit of one invaluable prayer, to discern what I can and cannot change. I learn to shoulder what I myself can commit to in some way at least, and pray for the courage and strength to help, and not to shy away, procrastinate, forget, not to turn a blind eye.

But I also learn to truly "surrender" and let go of the rest, the things I can't change—to humbly and realistically acknowledge my limits, to free myself from utopias and illusions about my own omnipotence, from overestimating and pointlessly overtaxing my own powers. In this way I can also rid myself of *specious* feelings of guilt, injustice, anger, impotence, worry, and stress vis-à-vis what I have to leave to God—since I'm not God—and to others, whom God will find to undertake those tasks. *Grant me, God, the courage and strength to change the things I can change, the patience and humility to endure what I can't change—and the wisdom to know the difference!*

Prayer is not a tranquilizing drug or an opportunity to snivel into God's apron. It is God's forge, in which we are to be, in the words of the gospel, remelted and forged into God's instrument, which, however, does not lose its freedom in God's hands, or responsibility for what it is used for.

Prayer is not a fanciful flight into the heavens and escape into the otherworld of our wishes. On the contrary, it draws our gaze back to the earth whenever we would simply like to gaze dreamily and passively into the clouds of our imaginings, projections, dreams, and utopias—exactly in the way that, on the day of the Ascension, the voice from heaven admonished the Lord's disciples, saying: Men of Galilee, why do you stand looking up toward heaven?[3] The same voice liberates us from all pious escapism and teaches us to stand firmly on the earth, *remain true to the earth*,[4] and realize that *the place on which we are standing is holy ground*.[5]

In prayer we become aware that this world—rather than Kant's "starry heavens above us and the moral law within us"—is the field in which God's treasure is hidden.[6] "The field is the world," as Jesus says to his disciples when explaining to them the parable of the sower.[7]

The field in which God is constantly at work and to which God constantly sends us to work is also our heart, of course, our life planted in this world. It is the ground that differs in terms of quality and how much it has been cultivated: if God's word falls among thorns, it won't germinate, if it falls on the stony ground of our hard "uncircumcised" hearts,[8] or into the shallow soil of our superficiality, it will die and be of no use.

If we are standing before a cross or icon when we pray, that symbol is not some magical or sacred object to be used for sorcery but a reminder (*anamnesis*), rousing us from the dream of narcissistic concentration on ourselves and leading us away from the temptation of soliloquy. Prayer is a dialogue in which we must not allow God's speech to be drowned out by the cascade of our beautiful, pious poems.

God's answer is not mysterious whispering into which we would constantly—whether naively or craftily—interweave our own answers, the ones we would like to hear in advance. God's "knocking on the wall" of our prison cell has nothing in common with the knocking on tables of spiritualist seances; or with divination from cards we have already been dealt, from birds' livers, from "chance opening of the Bible"; or with what we are persuaded to think by a preacher imitating the vulgar style of American televangelists.

God's answer is our own life, now calmly scrutinized with a certain detachment, in the light of God's word, before God's face. That is the text, whose often-intricate ciphers we solve using the gospel as a key (and, as was said before, we understand the gospel anew and ever more profoundly through our own life experience). Only in prayer and meditation is life, this fast-flowing stream of occurrences, transformed into *experience*, the fleeting fragments of words changed into meaningful text, and the red-hot iron of our sensations or life's misfortunes remolded in the forge of scripture. Yes, prayer is God's forge, not just a cozy slumber corner for noble souls; it is sometimes really hot!

I often talk about the "blessing of unanswered prayers." Not until people have confronted this experience are they on the real threshold of faith. If (often secretly) they have so far regarded God as some machine reliably fulfilling their orders, they now find out that "God doesn't work," that such a god, reliably functioning as a high-performance machine in their home, really *does not exist*. They would do well to reject such a god and such a religion. Only at this point do they have the opportunity to realize—although it is no broad highway that many will travel—that in faith and prayer it is more a matter of our trying to understand God's wishes, and having the strength, wisdom, and generous willingness to be able to give them precedence over our own wishes and demands.

Prayer is not submitting a list of our requirements but "exchanging concerns." Jesus says: Do not worry about what you will eat or drink, where you will live, or what you will wear—first concern yourself with the kingdom of God and God's righteousness and all the rest will be given you as well.[9] Of course this doesn't mean that I must undertake "the implementation of the kingdom" on my own and take the load of it off God's shoulders. The coming of God's kingdom is indeed God's work, not ours; whenever people have tried to implement heaven on earth using their own strength and resources, they have generally created hell on earth in a very short time. It also doesn't mean that I can pass the buck for my day-to-day livelihood onto the angels, or onto angels in human guise. (Many "piously carefree" individuals have tormented their neighborhood "angels," who have allowed these individuals to exploit them.)

It is a question of removing *anxiety* from the day-to-day concern of "putting food on the table," so that it does not totally occupy one's thoughts and take all one's energy, and ultimately it means that one should not be centered entirely on oneself. Our false concerns are always related to "having" (and not just material things), and they become truly harmful when "having" ceases to be a means and starts to be an end in itself.

The only way I can free myself from these false concerns and anxiety is if I really live according to a specific scale of values, and if I make it my priority to be open to everything that shatters the narrow horizon of our day-to-day concerns and, in particular, to be responsible *for recognizing and using* God's gifts.

Prayer and meditation are a workshop in which our fundamental decisions are formed and in which, after the fleeting froth of feelings has subsided, there matures our willingness to answer God—not like Adam, covered in excuses—but face to face.

Prayer and meditation are also, in the final analysis, a place of healing for our life's wounds.

No, I don't have in mind the "faith healing" that takes place during mass evangelization rallies at sports stadiums. I have always been of the view that the Christian faith belongs in stadiums more in the form of the martyrs who were eaten there by lions, rather than in the form of the lion, thoroughly keyed up on the drug of mass enthusiasm, that all too quickly devours the sober objections of critical reason. I have nothing against a dignified liturgy in open-air stadiums during a pope's travels or similar occasions. But if the megaphones blare out orders such as "If you believe in Christ, raise your hands, alleluia," which count on the forest of raised hands prompting the waverers to conform, and this is presented as conversion, then I would make the point that the Catholic liturgy at every mass contains the appeal *Sursum corda*, "Lift up your hearts" (not hands), and that the Christian tradition defines prayer as raising one's *heart* to God—an internal, not an external, motion.

To be sure, during the liturgy the priest also raises his hands, but this gesture is not in answer to an order from a megaphone as at the mass evangelization rallies, which are more reminiscent of unanimous voting by a show of hands in totalitarian parliaments. What will really get our bodies moving—legs for following and hands for work for God's kingdom—are transformed hearts, not a mood or inflamed emotions induced by mass suggestion. But hearts can't be transformed unless the heart is affected, or indeed wounded.

We are using "the heart" here in a biblical sense as the depth of the human being, not as the mere seat of feelings, emotions, and moods; "affecting the heart" implies a radical life change, not momentary excitement or emotion. In response to the rationalist and moralizing Enlightenment, which suppressed the life of the emotions, old Freud, the psychoanalysts, and after them humanistic psychology rightly sought to rehabilitate and liberate the emotions. But the total victory and enormous influence of humanistic psychology in all areas of Western culture, education, and society since the end of the 1960s caused the pendulum to swing to the opposite extreme. We live in a world in which *feelings* dictate and justify everything, and this one-sidedness is slowly corroding human character.

People who confuse *love* with emotional involvement *feel* justified in leaving their partners when they cease to *feel anything* toward them; people who confuse *faith* with pious emotional excitement start to regard themselves as atheists the moment their religious life has finally started to abandon its diapers and had a chance to mature; people who confuse *hope* with optimistic feelings are ripe for suicide when their optimistic illusions rightly fade—although this is precisely the moment for us to display the power of hope, *to give an account of our hope*, not of our moods.

Seen from above, from a theological perspective, faith, love, and hope are gifts from God, acts of God in pouring grace into our souls, "theological virtues." (I sometimes suspect that those who insist on looking *solely* from above are trying rather too hard "to look over God's shoulder.) When the same are seen from *below*, from our regular human perspective, these are acts of human decision and human freedom on the crossroads of possibilities: *Do I want or not want* to believe, love, and hope? If I want to believe, as Pascal knew well, I can *then* find many rational arguments for faith; if I don't want to believe, then I will spend the rest of my life happily coming across new reasons for my unbelief. Something similar applies to love and hope, and to forgiveness.

There is a contemporary Catholic exorcist whose books in many ways irritate me, although in many cases I have to admire his knowledge of human nature. He feels exasperated when people say they don't know whether they have forgiven some particular person or not. *If you want to forgive, then you've already forgiven them*, he tells them, and immediately adds: that does not mean, however, that the injuries that person caused you will immediately stop hurting, or that bitter memories will not return to you, or that you will suddenly be overcome with sympathy and tender emotions toward that person—the "healing of wounds" always requires lots of time.

It applies similarly to the matter of love, he adds. Love too is not simply a feeling, an emotional state of mind, but something quite different and much deeper. Love and hatred, he maintains, are matters of the *will*, not of feelings and attachments. If I have a liking for someone, it does not mean that I love them, and if I am not attracted to them, it doesn't mean I hate them: the Pharisees certainly didn't cause Jesus to have any liking for them, but he can't be said to have hated them.[10]

Love is when I wish another person well and am ready to *demonstrate* it as much as I am able; hate is when I wish them ill and am prepared to do them wrong whenever I have an opportunity to do so.

Maybe it is time to reawaken the will after a long hibernation when it was smothered in an avalanche of feelings. Nietzsche wasn't entirely wrong when he maintained that a passive believer must become a lion who freely says: *I will!*[11]

However, the difference is that the "I will" (or want) we have in mind here should not be a solitary king of the desert but should form itself in dialogue with God and our neighbors, as the response of our freedom to God's appeal, which is inscribed manifold in the wounds of our neighbors and our world.

Bodies

Quite a few years ago now, a couple in a certain German town petitioned for a crucifix to be removed from the wall of a classroom because their child could not be expected to look at such an ugly thing. The matter gradually turned into a public affair, which eventually led to a decision of the constitutional court in Karlsruhe that crucifixes were to be removed from all public schools. A few years later, following a widely publicized controversy about the wearing of the Muslim veil in schools, French legislators decided that in addition to the veil, the ("conspicuous") wearing of crosses around Christian necks, and the *kippa* on Jewish heads would be taboo in French schools. (Without fear or favor! A pity that the legislators weren't more schooled in the phenomenology of religion, or they would have known that these symbols play completely different roles in those religious systems and that the cross really doesn't have the same significance for the Christian as the veil for the Muslim woman—but so be it: when you cut down the forest, wood chips fly, as Uncle Joe Stalin used to say!) Around that same time the representatives of unified Europe passed a motion that the inclusion of the word *Christian* in the preamble of the draft Constitutional Treaty would be improper.

So be it! I'm sure that Europe will not be more or less Christian if this word is or isn't included in the Constitution; the Spirit that Christ promised *bloweth where it listeth* and certainly won't be stopped by official regulations or by zealous janitors in front of the gates of French or German schools. I probably wouldn't have joined the demonstration by Bavarian Catholics waving crosses in front of the courthouse, even though I understand the feelings of that generation of Germans, who have already once experienced the removal of crosses from classroom walls—and the next day their replacement by an official photograph of a man with a little moustache and a forelock across his forehead. It is not so much the actual removal of the cross that is interesting. After all, we Catholics are accustomed to covering the cross in churches during Lent; sometimes it is actually necessary to cover or remove certain symbols that we are so accustomed to that we cease to notice them, precisely so that we gain a deeper appreciation of their meaning in their absence. What is far more interesting is what appears in the space that is vacated. What kind of feast is being prepared for us by those who suggest that we "give up Christianity" as a fast? Maybe we will only appreciate the values of our faith when they are compared with what they are immediately replaced with.

I recalled that controversy about the ugliness of the cross and the unbearable sight of Christ's wounds a few years later on a visit to Berlin, when the city was awash with posters featuring photographs of corpses stripped of their skin. In the U-Bahn, on every corner, at the newsstands, everywhere there were these deliberately shocking advertisements for a traveling exhibition by an American entrepreneur displaying human remains with the title *Bodies*.

I didn't visit the exhibition, but the very idea of it and the fact that it could be organized seemed to me to be a sign so indicative of the state of contemporary culture and the secular relationship to death that I carefully studied all the available material, including photographs and promotional videos, and followed closely the extensive public debate that unfolded in the German media and elsewhere regarding the exhibition. I then reflected on all the arguments I had heard for and against in that debate. I was very interested by the initiative of one Berlin priest who said a requiem mass for the people who had been consigned, not to a grave, but to a display case as their place of no-rest, drooled over by sensation hunters and professional record breakers in the field of transcending the existing limits of what is morally and aesthetically acceptable.

Anthropologists have long recognized graveyards and the existence of a culture of burial as a sign of the beginnings of the

Homo sapiens species that distinguished it from its animal ancestors. Maybe the history of our culture and the human species ends where the distinction between the world of the living and the dead is erased, where the dead are no longer buried but placed on exhibition in showcases for high entrance fees, or maybe we are radically transformed into something else, which is unlikely to be nobler. In all events that exhibition seemed to me a sign that cannot be simply ignored or allowed to fade away along with the short-lived ballyhoo that the organizers deliberately provoke and welcome everywhere. You see, it tells us something important—and in my view alarming—about what is happening to human beings and our world today.

I would be very interested to know whether those parents who successfully protected their children from looking at Christ's ugly wounds on the cross blindfolded their children when passing these omnipresent pictures, or whether, on the contrary, they welcomed the exhibition as a triumph of awareness-raising, which has replaced religious obscurantism with its own symbols.

Before the year was out the *Bodies* exhibition arrived in Prague. It wasn't exactly the same exhibition as in Berlin, but its twin; the two American entrepreneurs had indulged in several mutual lawsuits, and of course they outbid each other in who could most dramatically break all taboos, pandering to the most morbid fantasies and raking in more money. Whereas in Berlin one of the cadavers was mounted on a skinned horse stripped of its skin, and the corpse of a pregnant woman was on display cut open with a dead embryo in her womb, in Prague his business rival amused the esteemed public with corpses arranged in the amusing poses of basketball players: the dead engaging in sport. There has to be a bit of humor, the exhibition's creator declared leeringly to Czech TV. I pondered for a moment on what another businessman might come up with to outdo these, now that the criterion of the acceptable has been shifted. How might he profit even more from human unfeelingness: maybe he could rent out or sell tastefully arranged corpses to householders as an attractive accessory for the postmodern home. . . .

Television, radio, the press, and highway billboards did their best to publicize the exhibition. The Prague city councilor who gave permission for it to be held in the very center of the city—for reasons I would not like to analyze—highly recommended it. The lines in front of the celebrated Lucerna exhibition hall got longer and the money came rolling in. I heard on the radio that increasing numbers of people were expressing a wish to be displayed like that after their death; it struck me that this kind of necrophilic exhibitionism merited inclusion in psychiatric textbooks under a separate diagnostic heading. Was I to voice my opinion about it all publicly or not?

So far nobody had spoken out against it—after all, the Czechs are a proverbially tolerant nation, particularly when they really oughtn't to be. (Only a few people were taken aback by the covert racist undercurrent of the exhibition—the dead people were all Chinese. Whether these were the bodies of executed political prisoners, as some maintained, or people in poverty who had simply sold their bodies—they were "just Chinese"; if that American entrepreneur had exhibited dead *Americans* in a similar manner, without heaps of legally notarized consent forms, he'd instantly be saddled with so many writs and court cases that he'd be paying lawyers to the end of his days, and probably would end up having to sell his own skin to a similar sideshow!) So was I to speak out?

When Madonna brought her latest show to Prague a few years ago, and during it was tied to a spectacularly illuminated cross, our hierarchy had protested it. Now they were silent.

On that particular occasion I had remained silent. Or rather I had prayed for Madonna, including during prayers of intercession at Sunday mass, that she be given the gift of a deeper understanding of the symbol she used so evocatively in her show—as well as the strength *to bear the cross* in her own life. All who take the sword will perish by the sword, Christ said. Maybe that also applies to the cross; if someone trifles with such a powerful symbol simply for effect, they might be surprised in the end to discover that the real cross, not the illuminated one, tends to be heavy.

Maybe the hierarchy were silent now because the Madonna incident had taught them that their protest simply served as publicity, boosting the attractiveness and ticket sales for the show they criticized, as well as a welcome pretext for the many people who would again portray the church as killjoy censors wanting to deprive people of the things they like.

I suspected that my protest would probably have a similar effect. I was also aware that I must not enter the ring with a moralizing wagging finger (even though it will be interpreted as such) but must instead use the weapons of irony and sarcastic humor. So I made a statement—and the responses were not long in coming.

"How dare you criticize such a splendid exhibition? Nobody's going to ban us from having our own opinions and tell us what we are supposed to like!" one indignant young man railed at me in an Internet debate. In his exasperation he had failed to notice that in his first sentence he was denying me the very right he claimed for himself in the second, namely, the right to hold and express one's own opinion. No, I do not have the slightest intention to command or prohibit what he is supposed feel or say, let alone what he is supposed to think; I am only too pleased when someone actually does think. Not only do I not demand the "closing of an exhibition"—it is up to their organizers and lawyers to judge to what extent they contravene the law—but I also don't demand that anyone should agree with me; what I want is to initiate a public debate, and if I have caused someone to think about the issue for themselves, even if they come to a completely different conclusion from my own, I am entirely satisfied. I have done my job!

Yes, a debate was indeed initiated, even though a slight majority of the views expressed—or at least it seemed to me for a while—were along similar lines to those of that indignant young man.

"How can you talk about the exhibition when you weren't at it?" But I know what was at the exhibition. If I had been there, my opinion would have been determined by my subjective feelings about the exhibition, just as my opponents argued that *they liked it*. But people's feelings, and what they like and don't like, depend on how they were brought up and how thick-skinned they are, whether someone of theirs died recently, or whether they had had lunch just before seeing the exhibition; that tells something about them, not about the exhibition itself! I didn't want to talk about the feelings that the exhibition might arouse in someone (naturally everyone has the right to their own feelings) but about the principle, whether or not dead bodies should be exhibited in that way.

If the organizers had decided to present the exhibition as "art," it would have been easier for them to silence their opponents, as postmodern aesthetics insist that it is impossible to define the boundaries between art and non-art, between the beautiful and the repulsive, between quality and trash. But corpses cannot be transported across national frontiers as works of art, so in order to circumvent the laws about the treatment of human remains, the crafty managers decided to pass off their sideshow as tool of scientific education. "They're not *bodies*, they're *exhibits*," the organizer of the Prague exhibition corrected me emphatically during a TV debate; so I asked him kindly to translate for the viewers who might not understand English the name of exhibition—*Bodies*—that was displayed all over the place.

"The exhibition is instructive!" Of course; if I had been present at a public execution or torture I would have undoubtedly have found it very instructive, and I would have discovered lots of interesting details about the human psyche and how the human body reacts; but that criterion does not justify executions or torture. For the teaching of anatomy there are anatomical museums, where there really are exhibits, but such museums tend to be empty. Anyone wanting to learn about dying and death can volunteer, for a while at least, to assist in a hospice or a hospital for the chronically sick—but there are not many who line up to do so.

No, the crowds didn't throng the box office out of scientific interest, and the ones who raked in millions from that box office were well aware of it: they were causing a sensation and breaking another taboo. But not all taboos are meaningless, and not every transgression of boundaries is beneficial.

"Who is the church to talk? It displays relics, doesn't it! Haven't you seen those saints in churches in crystal coffins?" Yes, I've seen them, and, as the point of a well-known anecdote has it: there's no comparison.[1] I'm no great fan of holy relics; if I was ever canonized I'd prefer to be food for the worms than to be portioned out for relics like my patron saint Thomas Aquinas; I'd hate to look down from heaven and see bits of my body wandering around dusty sacristies and occasionally kissed by precisely the kind of old women who couldn't stand me when I was alive. And yet I have knelt on several occasions with reverence before the coffin of one of my favorite female saints: she lies there in a nun's habit with a mask over her face. If they were to skin her, place a volleyball in her hands, photograph her for highway billboards everywhere, drive her from town to town like an attraction, and charge money for it, it really would be something rather different. Is it really so hard to distinguish between the two things?

"And have you seen the ossuaries in the crypts of baroque churches?" Yes, I've seen them too. And although my taste, and probably the taste of most present-day Christians, is rather different from that of the baroque—in this matter, at least—I am able to read the sign over the door and understand it: *Memento mori!* Put aside your pride, and don't feel superior to others—you are approaching a place where we will all be equal! Make wise use of fleeting time and don't put off your good intentions, because when you will be like the ones here, it will be too late to carry them out! These are the messages of the baroque crypts. And what is the message of this exhibition? "Just look at all the things I've been willing to contravene in order to earn big money and get the attention of the press for a week!"

Or could it be that the message of this exhibition—irrespective of the superficial intentions of its organizers—is something more profound, but also more appalling?

Those crowds didn't stand in line for hours just because there was a lot of talk about it on TV and in the pub. People are naturally drawn to the mystery of death and everything related to it. At one point in his *Republic*—as if predicting the exhibition two and a half millennia later—Plato writes about the ambivalent feelings of people seeing human corpses beneath the city walls; they know they ought not look, but they can't help it; they are drawn to it, and it is "stronger than they are."

The alluring fascination of death and its attributes relates to the fact that in death we are standing at the gates of Mystery and are not allowed to look beyond its walls. Atheists, Christians, Jews, and Muslims are only believers in their version of the interpretation of what will come after. No one will ever provide real proof or disproof of it, but human inquisitiveness doesn't like waiting. And so regarding everything directly connected with death we long to at least glimpse a ray from the gates that have opened for someone else before immediately closing impenetrably behind them.

In a world where the ubiquitous industry of cheap entertainment gradually absorbs everything into itself, trivializing and profaning everything, and divesting it of any depth, death was maybe the last island of mystery, arousing not fear, maybe, but awe. And lo here is death itself dragged into an entertainment sideshow! For a hefty fee you can gawk at it to your heart's content, and you can cheerfully show your kids (who pay half-price!) dead people playing volleyball, displayed like monkeys in the cages of zoos, in this showcase of materialism taken to absurd lengths. What did they actually want to see, these voyeurs of *total striptease*, in which the dead are stripped not only of their last remnant of dignity but also of their skin, if not death itself, in an elegantly coquettish gesture, tossing off the last veil of its mystery?

"There's nothing here!" the materialist anatomists of the early modern era shouted mockingly at those seeking a soul, when they first cut human corpses into little pieces in public shows. "There's nothing here!" the naturalists shouted from their dissecting rooms and laboratories at those seeking God, when they were anatomizing the evolution of the universe and the human species with the knives and scissors of their theories. "There's nothing here!" the managers of this morbid circus—in which death itself, naked and trivialized, is transformed into an exhibit and commodity—shout at those seeking the ultimate meaning of life. It's just no big deal at all!

In this world God is nothing—and we have to reduce ourselves to nothing if we want to encounter God equally naked. But you didn't have *this* in mind, did you, Meister Eckhart!

When I saw photos of both exhibitions, I said to myself: that must be what hell looks like—total *depersonalization* of the human being. No hissing cauldrons or souls being fried, no screaming from torture chambers, as the baroque fantasy imagined it. Instead this silence—not the meditative silence of churches or Christian cemeteries but the total absence of any communication: these dead persons have no names, no faces, nothing. There is nothing to indicate their life story. In a certain sense that manager of the exhibition was right when he said they weren't really bodies—they are not bodies as an expression of personal identity (which is why Christianity insists on "the resurrection of the *body*"!), just anonymous *exhibits*. People have been turned into objects, things to be displayed and exhibited. Interesting—for some instructive, for others entertaining, maybe. Bodies without faces cease to be pictures of the soul. They reflect nothing, they allude to nothing else. They are truly immodestly "naked"—without a name or a story. They are a number in a catalogue, as the concentration camp prisoners were.

The naked body on the cross has its story—it is fundamentally an allusion, chock-full of meaning (as witness all those who have meditated in front of it for two thousand years); it is an *icon*—an open window directing the meditative gaze toward the mystery of the Father and the mystery of human suffering.[2] If this sign no longer means anything, if it no longer speaks to us because we don't know how to listen to it, or are unwilling to, if it has become for us simply a conventional accessory to the devotional corner of the home or a "cultural heritage" logo, and for others "an ugly thing," then perhaps it is natural that the call for it to be taken down and disposed of will prevail. But there is one thing I fear: that the vacated space might be filled by faceless and nameless bodies.

Our ancestors prayed in churches before the cross with the likeness of a man with a pierced heart: Make our hearts like unto Thine! If sideshows of morbid exhibits and all-consuming mindless entertainment become the temples of the future, it will be probably hard to escape another danger: inside them we ourselves might start slowly and stealthily begin to resemble *things*, interchangeable exhibits, commodities, worthless samples.

10

A Little Place for Truth

A few years ago I took part one Sunday in a midday debate on Czech Television with the deputy chairwoman and vice-chairman of the two biggest political parties. When it was all over and I was alone for a moment on the back staircase with the vice-chairman, I asked him a question that I knew would probably cause him to regard me as an alien from outer space who had blundered into a world of experts and experienced operators; I was nevertheless curious to see what he would reply. "Mr. Vice-Chairman, as we are just the two of us here: you do realize, don't you, that what you have been declaring to the camera the whole time just isn't the truth." The politician gave me a look that was a mixture of pity and scorn, like a well-armed Goliath confronted by cheeky little boy who had happened to be momentarily barring his way. "The truth?" He repeated the word after me with such aversion, as if I'd dared to say something improper to him. "Sir, I'm talking to my people and she's talking to hers." In other words, we politicians, experienced professionals, naturally tell the people who are our potential voters what they want to hear. Our concern is to get their votes and ensure we keep getting paid as members of parliament and enjoy the opportunities democracy offers us. After all, don't we pay lots of money for opinion polls? What is true and what the real facts are doesn't interest us at all. That's totally irrelevant. Someone who doesn't understand that shouldn't get in the way of us, who are experts on the basic rules of politics. Such a naive, muddle-headed person shouldn't be surprised if he gets trodden on fairly soon.

I realized that a whole lot of people would applaud his statement, either because they adhere to this ideology and practice it themselves, and have enough courage or cynicism to admit it without scruples, or because they regard themselves as "realists," who accept that this is really the way politics operates and have given up trying to imagine that it could ever be any different, let alone doing something about it themselves. There's no way of changing it, is there?

Democracy—like the church—will always be imperfect, being created by people with all their frailties, faults, and bad inclinations. I have warned in the past against the pathos of moral rigorism and idealism that abandons democracy because it is the rule of the people and not of angels. Why should a saint occupy the seat of the vice-chairman, or at least someone less cynical and arrogant? Aren't politicians simply a mirror image of the citizens who voted for them, after all? Shouldn't society, which is always grumbling and constantly berating its political representatives, recognize itself in them instead?

Have I the right to be offended by the behavior of politicians after having briefly considered—for about three years—whether to go into politics myself and try to offer a different style and different values before finally deciding not to? Haven't I thereby joined those who have given up the struggle, if I am no longer willing—as I considered for a while—to abandon my beloved service at the altar, my university chair, and this writing desk in my summer hermitage in favor of service to society, even for just five years, because I want in this final third of my life struggle to save my time and strength for the truly fundamental *unum necessarium*?

In all these reflections I was constantly being distracted by the memory of that politician's scornful tone. His dishonoring of the word *truth* stung me like the slap ultimately inflicted on the one who said: *I am the truth*, the way, and the life.

That evening I read again the Easter story in John's Gospel. It occurred to me that Pilate's question "What is truth?" could be pronounced in the precisely same manner as that of the vice-chairman. The thought also struck me whether Jesus returned after the night of the cross and tomb and revealed his wounds partly to demonstrate that the power of Goliath and Pilate's followers does not always have to have the last word, and that their mockery of those who have not abandoned questions of truth might be somewhat premature.

But why did Christ not show it "to all the people," as scripture says, only to those he had summoned to be *his witnesses*? Why didn't he show himself to the Pilates and the vice-chairmen? Maybe because he left that task to us. He empowered those of us who claim allegiance to him to be, like him, "witnesses to the truth" in the circumstances where we find ourselves—with all that entails. And what that entails can be read about precisely in the story of Easter.

Of course not everyone who sets out on this path has to end up on a cross, but they can be sure that the *foolishness of the cross* will *stigmatize* them in the eyes of vice-chairmen, chairmen, cynics, pragmatists, and "realists," who have given in to the "inevitable"! There are not just the spectacular stigmata that shine out to us in gold from the paintings of outstanding saints. There are also everyday stigmata that we must get used to and accept as something normal, as the inevitable accoutrements of Christian discipleship. The stigmata of those who "did not obey the party line" and conform, of those who step out of line.

Yes, the world in which the vice-chairman thinks about things *is crucified to me and I to it.* This doesn't mean that I must immediately demonize his world, nor at all that I must fear it and entirely shun it. I cannot even totally separate myself from it mentally and physically—we all live here in one world, and our private and group worlds, the worlds of our values, dreams, and interests, overlap and will continue to do so for as long as "this world" exists. We are *in the world*, but insofar as we belong to Christ, we are not *of the world*,[1] and that means that we cannot and must not conform to what Pilate and the vice-chairmen predicate on, or to the way they approach truth and power. For them power is sacred, and truth is of no account and ludicrous; for us power must be divested of its sacred aura, but the truth must remain sacred.

If the vice-chairmen want to eliminate the question of truth (so that no one should doubt the self-legitimizing sacredness of power), they are going about it now very cleverly. If we speak about truth, they reproach us with taking the arrogant and haughty position of possessors of the truth and claim that we are in reality dangerous agents of totalitarianism, while they are defending freedom and democracy from us.

Are they not part of democratic politics, and isn't their power legitimized by the number of votes they received in elections and by the strength of the majority opinion that they represent (having previously taken enormous efforts to create and manipulate it)? What gives us a mandate to stand in their way and have the gall to question their actions in any way? "There is nothing you can do or say that we don't like, so long as we are in power," is their message to us; "The most you can do is to wait for the next election, which will prove once again what an insignificant minority you are, and how splendidly we'll manage to express the thinking of people who prefer not to think!" After all we have the means, and we know that if there is any risk of people starting to *think* we can always throw an impactful slogan into the ring. "You speak on behalf of the 1 percent of your friends who don't sustain my business," the owner of a successful commercial TV station once told me.

But even here the vice-chairmen lie: we do not regard ourselves as "possessors of the truth." We ask about the truth—and that question has a subversive power vis-à-vis the monopoly of power. The political mandarins rightly suspect this and fear it.

Jesus refused to let people on the streets of the world call him Messiah and king—not because it wasn't true but because his messianic role and kingship had to be revealed only in the drama of the Passion, because there they would show themselves to be what they truly were: the paradox of the *power of the powerless*, as a claim that deviates from the claims of kings, vice-chairmen, and messiahs that the world offers; as a claim that questions them and their claims. When Pilate asks about truth, Jesus—unlike all the "possessors of truth"—offers no theory, slogan, or definition, no ideology; he remains silent.

But in his silence, his powerlessness, and his cross (perhaps for the first and last time) truth is revealed, uncontaminated by connections or compromises with power or its interests. As we said before, here stands Christ-Truth as a mirror, in which the world, man, and God are seen as they really are. Here is no claim to "total power," unlike the totalitarian ideologies and regimes of this world. This mirror provides no answer like the answers in the various political and religious catechisms of all hues; it simply allows us to see[2]—and leaves open the question of how we interpret that vision and how we deal with it (with ourselves).

And the critical questions we put to power are more of a mirror. We leave it up to power itself if it wants to look in the mirror or break it. "I'm not interested in the way things are, I just seek approval and collect votes."

But if the vice-chairmen "collect votes," we mustn't allow them to collect either our vote or, above all, our voice: "the voice crying in the wilderness" raising its unremittingly unpopular questions. Democracy itself and its mechanisms as such are not capable of ensuring a free society: they can *help* to ensure it, but only where people in society think about and freely discuss the truth.

No, we are not "possessors of the truth"—and our faith actually forbids us to present ourselves as anything of the kind. If we believe that "Christ is the truth" (and that only he had the right to say of himself, "I am the truth") and we confess that "we believe in Christ," we thereby admit that we are not Jesus Christ, and we are not the truth—and for that reason we must resist the temptation to play at "the Truth" and at holding a monopoly of the truth.[3]

We don't possess Christ. Neither the object of faith nor faith itself is property; rather, it is a commitment. Christ commits us to following him, seeking the truth and persevering. "For as long as we live on this earth we cannot possess God but must seek him," wrote Martin Luther. "We must always seek him and search for him and ever keep seeking him. . . . For not he that starts to seek but he that 'perseveres' in seeking 'to the end will be saved' (Matthew 10:22; 24:13), one who begins his seeking all over again, ever seeking again what he has found. For he that does not go forward in God's way goes backward. And he that does not persist in seeking loses what he has found, for there is no standing still in the way of God."[4]

Equating ourselves with the Truth and pretending to be possessors of the truth is as much a sin as ceasing to care about the truth
and defecting to the cynics' camp.

If the church and individual Christians are to fulfill their prophetic role—standing in the way of power when it scorns the very
question of the truth—they must not, for a moment, stop asking
themselves self-critically and humbly to what extent they themselves stand in the truth and understand it. Truth doesn't only place
demands on others, it places demands above all on us.

The outward confrontation with those who scorn the truth and
the injuries we might incur in the process should not deter us from
our inward struggle to be truthful ourselves or from diligently asking ourselves to what extent we ourselves are humbly open to the
truth. *Disputes without and fears within* is the way St. Paul described
it.[5] This is, however, the normal state of "a warrior of God" if he is
not to become a "religious terrorist" (albeit in an elegant Western
guise, maybe).

"Truth is not a topic for discussion"—I heard that dreadful
statement not from a representative of political power but from a
representative of our church.[6] But what else should we discuss, if
not the truth? If the church starts (or doesn't stop) considering the
truth entrusted to it as its property instead of its commitment, it
cannot fulfill its prophetic role in the world, and it will have lost
every battle against cynical political power in advance, not just
physically and politically, but also morally. At that moment it is
a matter of "power versus power" (and in the end they are indis-
tinguishable, like the animals and people at the end of Orwell's
Animal Farm)—and the one that is bound to lose in that conflict is
truth itself.

The Croatian theologian Miroslav Volf, whom I have quoted
on many occasions in this book, wrote about truth and the Christian ministry of "bearing witness to the truth" one of the most
beautiful things I have ever heard on this topic from a theologian.
He writes *inter alia*: "'The truth shall make you free,' said Jesus.
Free for what? . . . Free to make journeys from the self to the other

and back and to see our common history from their perspective as well as ours, rather than closing ourselves off and insisting on the absolute truth of our own perspective; free to live a truthful life and hence be a self-effacing witness to truth rather than fabricating our own 'truths' and imposing them on others."[7]

Yes, the vice-chairmen have a huge part of "public space" at their disposal, in which to present their version of the world in many different ways. Nevertheless, we must not "lose our voices" at those moments when we must point out, at least in the form of unwelcome questions, that there are also other ways of considering things.

"There's a little place for truth everywhere in this world" runs an old Czech hymn. Where is that little but "strategically important" place? From where can we again and again *undermine* those dangerous totalitarian statements of cynical, unscrupulous power, if only in the form of questions about the truth that cannot be silenced? That place is in our faith, insofar as it has itself resisted the temptation to become an ideology—in our trust in the truth, which we must never abandon, however many times it is wounded, mocked, disappointed, and crucified. It is a little place, an island in the world of Goliaths, that we must defend come what may.

No, faced with the Goliaths of power, as the vice-chairman knew all too well, I don't even have the pebbles and slingshot of our father David. The only weapon I have against the temptation to capitulate and join the cynics, "realists," and their fellow-travelers is my faith—and a wounded faith to boot.

It is not an ideology that could be a means of achieving power, it is not a reliable recipe for victory in the arena of competing interests. It is a *way*, and one, moreover, that leads in one form or another to the cross and points to the cross. And the fact that the cross, that defeat of the truth, is not the final victory of the cynical establishment vice-chairmen and the other deputies of the Pilates, Herods, and Caiaphases in all epochs is only given us as hope. We have no other means of demonstrating it to the world—"accounting for our hope"—but by living ourselves in the spirit of that hope.

Is there some way of using this vulnerable and constantly wounded faith to help heal the world around us? Healing the world is a task for the Messiah. If we were to try to undertake that task with our own resources, it would indicate we were infected with messianism and megalomania, which have already caused so much harm and so many tragedies in the course of history.

But if we reject messianism—and we have already seen that this is an act of humility, which is an integral part of our belief in the Messiah—we need not descend into indifference, cynicism, and apathy. On the contrary: only then can we soberly perceive the task prepared for each of us.

Healing the world means "enlarging the place of truth." The supreme "place of truth" is the Kingdom of God, God alone in his power, to be revealed at the end of time. That "little place of truth" is, as we have already said, our faith—and through it, and in it, Christ himself.

We aren't Christ—but we are charged with doing his work in all humility. Insofar as we do not present just ourselves, insofar as we do not constantly pursue just our own advantage and our own selfish (private or group) interests, and insofar as we do not promote only our own power and our own glory, insofar as in our own hearts we go on asking after the truth in the thoroughfares of the world, we represent Christ. Truth is *the way* and the life; complacent inaction is spiritual death. Only insofar as we renounce our own proud (private, national, political, or ecclesiastical) messianism do we participate in his messianic mission to heal and free the world by the truth.

11

Veronica and the Imprint of the Face

When the Resurrected One came to the disciples, men who were still in the grip of fear, grief, and disillusionment, dejected by the shadow of the cross and their own failure in having abandoned Jesus and fled in a cowardly fashion, he spoke to them first in the language of his wounds. And what about the women?

They didn't abandon him or run away. They accompanied him on his way of the cross to the very last moment—and they were the first to find the open tomb, the open womb of the Easter morning mystery. The gospel records the names of some of them. The medieval mystery plays speak about the three Marys, and the countless pictures and sculptures depicting the Crucifixion down the ages feature two women in particular—the virgin Mother and also the former prostitute from Magdala, from whom Jesus drove out seven devils, the woman who had enormous love for him and was very close to his heart.[1] The Gospels, and John's Gospel most explicitly, acknowledge that Mary Magdalene became the "apostle of the apostles," and the first appearance of the Risen One was reserved for her.[2]

Jesus's insistent "Don't touch me! Don't cling to me!," resisting the Magdalene's embrace, is in striking contrast to his invitation to Thomas: "Reach out your hand and put it in my side." But nothing is said about whether Thomas really did touch Jesus's wounds. Jesus's words to Mary Magdalene (and likewise his "walking through a closed door" and his sudden disappearance at Emmaus) would seem to be intended to protect the reader from a crudely "materialist" interpretation of the Resurrection, which might arise from a superficial reading of the scene with Thomas (one that fundamentalists defend and that we repeatedly warn against in this book).[3] In opposition to the naively fundamentalist concept of the physicality of resurrection, the Gospels, traditional faith, and the theology of the church insist that the body of the Resurrected One is a "transformed body," that in this respect *body* means above all the unmistakable identity of the person and that the Resurrection and the Resurrected One are part of an eschatological mystery that enters this world and its history *through the gate of faith and hope*, which they also arouse and fulfill. We cannot trivialize them by simply categorizing them among the *bruta facta* of our world and by trying fatuously to support and secure them by overeager proofs of our reason and apologetic pamphlets. Easter morning is the dawn of that glorious day that we will only fully wake up into from our own sleep of death. Now we touch it only through our faith, and our faith is illuminated by its rays only insofar as it is a "gift of grace."

Our belief in Christ's resurrection relies on the testimony of witnesses into whose ranks we are invited and drawn by faith and grace. These were not and are not "eyewitnesses" (there were no eyewitnesses of the Resurrection event). We join them as those who are ready to testify through our lives that Jesus does not belong just to the past but that we relate to him as our future and demonstrate in the present moment that he is present in the world and *alive* for us, in us, and through us.

But even this gift we have in "earthenware vessels"—our faith also remains at the same time a human act, a pilgrim's faith, which, during our journey through this world and in this body, cannot fully emerge from the twilight of doubt, nor free itself completely from the limitations of our reason, language, experience, and notions.

Indeed, in this world even the most passionate love and yearning, like the Magdalene's embrace, will always be reminded not to seek *by* touch to fully remove the veil of mystery and cling to it like an object to be possessed. Just as the brightness of Mount Tabor led immediately to the downward path to the valley of the everyday world, and indeed to the darkness of Gethsemane, so also the encounter with the Resurrected One, however joyous it might be, cannot be "held onto" and stored in our treasure chest of certainties,

among the certainties and treasures of this world. It is a certainty
of a different order—deeper and also more subtle and vulnerable,
like a flame to be protected on a windy journey; we also cannot retain Jesus's resurrection by suggesting that we "build three dwell-
ings for it" here.[4] He is still on a journey, he is on his way to the
Father, he is *the way* to him—and he doesn't even want us to retain
him, he wants us to walk with him.

There is one woman who is not mentioned in the Gospels
but is familiar to legends and the deep intuition of popular piety,
which even devotes one of the fourteen stations of the cross to her.
Veronica, the woman who lent Jesus her veil to wipe the blood and
sweat from his facial wounds, received for posterity a memento
that has imprinted itself astonishingly deeply onto the history of
Christian imagination: Jesus imprinted the image of his face onto
Veronica's veil.

Countless legends would recount the subsequent fortunes of
that image, and the "likeness not made by hand" not only would be
exhibited, conserved, copied, and venerated throughout the world
but would become an important element in the theology of Christian art. An icon—as opposed to an idol, which is "a god fashioned
by human hands using human imagination," a projection of human
wishes—is a "window" opening the world and matter to a promised
eschatological reality, to things that "no eye has seen" (1 Corinthians 2:9), nor can the eye be fully satisfied in this world, because
here "we see in a mirror, dimly" (1 Corinthians 13:12). It is a chink
in the locked door of mystery, a place letting in enough light to
allow our world to be seen as a veil of the Face, whose smile gives
us enough encouragement not to falter even when we must walk the
valley of the longest shadows.

But for Christians the world is not "the veil of Maya"; it is not
just an illusion; matter is not simply darkness, the body is not just
a tomb, the earth is not an abyss and a trap. Herein lies the fundamental difference between the Christian understanding of reality
and the "material world" and the Oriental, Platonic, gnostic, and
idealistic concepts thereof. The world, matter, and the body are

God's good creation (about which the Creator himself declared that "it was good");[5] the body is an "expression of the soul" rather than its prison. The matter of this world can be sacramental materials, a real and effective sign of God's presence. The face of Christ was imprinted forever onto this world—but only those who spread out a veil of compassion and mercy for those who bear a cross will receive its seal.

So many people have wanted to hear the *name* that God refused to reveal to Moses from the burning bush,[6] so many people have wanted to see his face even though he promised his servant that he would see him only "from behind" as if in passing.[7] The people of the first covenant preserved the name and face of the Lord in the mystery of inaccessibility. Christianity proclaims to the world the name and face of the Son as a seal that the Father himself placed on history, as the Word, with which he himself broke his silence.

But in doing so Christian faith does not belittle, deplete, or disturb the mystery of the Father. It does not lower the threshold of the sanctuary or make it "easy" or cheap to reach. The name of the Son cannot be used as an incantation. Jesus himself warned against fatuously calling to him, "Lord, Lord!";[8] he wants us to *perform deeds* like the ones he performed—nay even greater.[9] If we were to use the face of the Son simply as a magic symbol on our standards, as our group "logo," or as an eye-catcher on publicity posters, it would become a profane caricature.

Jesus's real face will be seen only by Veronica and those who will follow her. Where *passio* (suffering) is met with *compassio* (compassion), the one who entered the depths of suffering will imprint a seal of authenticity on the compassion, he will "sign it in his blood," so to speak.

Jesus's face cannot be carved into the marble of hardened hearts. It is to be found among the *merciful*, among *the pure in heart, for they shall see God* and receive mercy.[10] The merciful anticipate the "beatific vision," the eschatological resting place in the radiance of God's face: they see Christ's face in those who suffer, and they themselves reveal it to the world by showing them compassion and love, and helping them.

If an icon (including reverence for it) is "authentic" and does not degenerate into an idol and idolatry—the portrayal of God being forbidden in scripture—it must be transparent and "translucent" in two ways. It must first turn the believer's eyes and heart away from the mundane, material, and visible world (and *through* it) to the Invisible and what cannot be portrayed. But then it turns them back to the world, so that in his light (and *through* him) we might see the face of God in the world in the faces of those who suffer.

An icon is a window to God, although it is still hidden by a veil through which only God's light shines. An icon teaches us to perceive the world as a "symbol," as a translucent veil both concealing and revealing God's mystery; it teaches us to value the world for its "translucence." And Christ's face as it was captured by Veronica's veil, that is, the face of every suffering individual if we capture it through a gesture of compassion and help, is precisely the place in the world where the light of God's presence shines through with the greatest radiance.

It is said that countless saints, both canonized and uncanonized, bore on their bodies stigmata, the visible signs of Christ's wounds, imprinted into the skin and flesh of their bodies. Veronica is the first fruits of those who inwardly conserve the imprint of Christ's wounds, his face, wounded and bruised by the malice of all ages, because they "removed the veil from their hearts" and gave it to the afflicted.

Painfully exasperated with his compatriots for not accepting Christ as the Messiah, Paul wrote of them that a veil lay over their minds like the veil that covered Moses's face when it was glowing after his encounter with the Lord.[11] But the faces of those who have turned to Christ, "seeing the glory of the Lord as reflected in a mirror," are transformed into his image through the power of the spirit.

Let us beware of interpreting these words in a triumphalist fashion, as a mechanical demarcation of the external boundaries between Christians and Jews. How many of us who had the water of baptism poured over our heads have really turned to Christ, particularly to Christ in the needy, to such an extent that our faces truly mirror the light of his face amid the gloom of the world?

And wasn't it precisely that great Jewish thinker Emmanuel Lévinas who reminded twentieth-century people that we will see God *in the face of the other*, whose nakedness and vulnerability calls, "You shall not kill"? And doesn't the spirit of the gospel blow through the ancient Jewish legend in which a rabbi sends his pupils among the wounded and leprous outside the gates of Jerusalem to find the Messiah hiding among them and waiting to be recognized? The sign by which they would identify him was as follows: they would all be bandaging their own wounds except for one who would be bandaging the wounds of others. That would be him, the Messiah.

Even when we eagerly say, "Lord, Lord," and even when his holy image hangs on the walls of our homes, perhaps a veil lies over our hearts, and until we remove it, like Veronica, we will not go outside the city walls and truly become his pupils in the dressing stations of a leprous world.

Let us add one more meditation to reflection on the feminine aspect of Easter. There is another picture profoundly associated with the time of silence between the afternoon of Good Friday and Easter morning: the pietà, the penultimate station of the cross and the subject of countless works of art (from the emotionally fervent work of folk carvers to the somewhat heartless beauty of Michelangelo's *Pietà* at the entrance to the Vatican basilica)—the mother with the dead body of her son on her lap. When I am standing in front of these depictions I can't help sensing their "vibrations" when I think of what this image is "saturated" with: how many mothers—particularly in the wars of the past millennium— must have knelt in front of them, injecting all their pain into the scene and seeking within it the strength to accept their own lot.

"*In gremio matris sedet sapientia Patris*"—In the lap of the mother lies the wisdom of the Father—is a sentence accompanying many medieval depictions of the Madonna with the child in her lap. Mary herself is perceived by mystics as *Sapientia*, a symbol of that mysterious wisdom which, according to the Wisdom books of the Old Testament, accompanied God during his work of creation, the wisdom that "played before him" and was a symbol of the "Shekhinah," the cloud of God's mysterious presence, beauty, and power. But she is also *Sedes Sapientiae*, "the throne of (God's) wisdom." For medieval theologians Mary was a symbol of humanity, of human nature, reason, and hence also philosophy and "natural theology"—what forms the "base," the soil, the throne for the revealed Wisdom, to which theology is dedicated. *Gratia supponit naturam*, the order of grace presupposes the order of nature, Thomas Aquinas maintained; theology presupposes philosophy; the seed of God's Word presupposes the open soil of humanity—and it is all symbolized by Mary: her virginity and openness, her womb and her *Fiat*—Let it be with me according to your word! (The fact that for the Middle Ages philosophy was *ancilla theologiae*, the handmaid to theology, does not mean it is some servant performing an inferior task—it has the same status as Mary, *the handmaid of the Lord*, who enables God, by the openness of her *Fiat*, to perform his work freely while fully respecting human freedom.)

Before the body of the Son is laid in the womb of the earth, it rests for a while in the lap of the Mother. Mary symbolizes the earth: just as at the beginning of the work of creation the earth was *without form and void* but above its waters *hovered the spirit of God*,[12] so at the beginning of the work of redemption the same Spirit came upon Mary[13] and "overshadowed" her as it had veiled the Ark of the Covenant. But where was that Spirit—the Comforter (*Parakleitos*)[14]—in the hour beneath the cross? The hour of Pentecost had not yet arrived.

The "King of the Jews" rests on the "throne" of Mary's lap—the Wisdom of the Father, which its foes, the clever and powerful of this world, can now mock to their hearts' content as foolishness. Is it possible to imagine a more absurd scene? Just as "the exile of the Shekhinah" is a concept in Jewish mysticism, Christian devotion similarly experiences this moment—the Son is dead, the Father is silent, the Spirit has not yet descended; the hopes of the morning when the *Shekhinah* will return are covered in the darkness of pain and in the heart of the one known in the liturgy as "the Morning Star" (*stella matutina*).

"Drop down, ye heavens, from above, and let the skies pour down righteousness—*Let the earth be opened and send forth a Savior*." This verse of Isaiah, which we usually associate with Advent, also has a profoundly paschal meaning.

The mystic commentaries on the mystery of Holy Saturday reflect on what happened in the "depths of the earth," in "hell," to which the Savior descended through his suffering, and where his cross became a weapon piercing the gates of darkness. But what was taking place in the depths of the mother's heart at that moment, in the hell of her pain?

The Easter suffering of the mother is described in the Latin hymn *Stabat mater*, which has inspired countless splendid musical works. But it is precisely when I am listening to these works that I can't help wondering whether this is not an aestheticization of suffering. Isn't beauty one of the ways by which we seek to blunt the cutting edge of pain?

Are we not closer to the mystery of the pietà, the penultimate station of the cross, at places through which history's way of the cross passes, the way of the afflicted of past and present, where the face of the earth is truly blood-sodden like Mary's lap beneath the cross?

I think about it in the Church of the Holy Sepulcher in Jerusalem, where the places of Jesus's death and resurrection are displayed—the church, which those who came to "liberate the Holy Sepulcher from the hands of the infidels" filled with blood up to their horses' bridles.

I think about it at Hiroshima on that early summer morning—on the Feast of the Transfiguration in a bright cloud on Mount Tabor—when along with believers from seven religions we mark the anniversary of the day when the city was veiled in the deadly cloud of the atomic explosion.

I think about it in Auschwitz in the cell of Maximilian Kolbe, on the execution ground and in the gas chambers, and in the chapel of the Carmelite nuns where prayers are said constantly for reconciliation, repentance, peace, and the healing of the world.

I think about it at "Ground Zero" in Manhattan, where what remains of the proudly raised fingers of the twin towers is an open wound in the ground, and where we clasp our hands in prayer.

But how many scars and open wounds that no one knows about, and about which no one comes to stand in reverence, are borne by the face of "Mother Earth"?

Many of them are of a kind that we are unable to prevent or confront. They come from areas that are truly beyond our control and out of range of our power. Sometimes we don't know about them, or don't see them, or don't want to see them; at other times the pages of the newspapers and TV screens are so saturated with them that we are unable to take them in, and we instantly forget them like yesterday's sports results (which accompany them).

Evil will triumph over us not only when and if we adopt its methods but also if we become accustomed to it. Among the most dangerous sins of our times is that many *confuse something frequently repeated with the normal* and "normal" with the norm; as a result, a frequently repeated phenomenon ceases to be evil in the eyes of the public, in the way that "an oft-repeated lie becomes the truth." But a moral code cannot be supplanted by statistics.

It is therefore important that every instance of suffering, distress, injustice, or injury caused by evil be treated as a unique case and not allowed to become an anonymous statistic.

Someone must keep vigil like Mary, someone must take these sorrows "in their lap," someone must prevent them being forgotten, someone must "keep them in their heart" even if they don't understand them—someone must carry them in their lap and heart from the shadow of Calvary to the dawn of Easter morning.

Wounds Transformed

Where are the dressing stations or our world? Certainly not just in those remote exotic locations or battlefields, illuminated for a while by TV cameras, where our romanticism might draw us. They are all around us.

"Look at my hands and my feet," Christ says today, gazing at all those who suffer or are wounded, near and far. "Touch me and see; for a ghost does not have flesh and bones as you see that I have."[1]

"Men and women are flesh and bone, hands and feet, the pierced side of Christ—his mystic body," adds the author concealed by the pseudonym Moine de l'Eglise d'Orient.[2] "In them we can achieve the reality of resurrection by our actions." He challenges us to see Christ not only in the socially needy, the sick, the poor, and the abandoned, but above all in people who are remote from us and that we don't like: "Christ is imprisoned once more in many of those men and women—in wicked and criminal people. Free him by recognizing him quietly and silently and you will invoke him in them."

These are difficult, demanding words. Who can listen to them? And who has the courage to put them into practice, or at least try? We are accustomed from many sermons to being challenged to help people in social distress, and maybe we do so from time to time. There are not too many sermons about loving one's enemies—and when there are, one often has the embarrassing feeling that neither the preacher nor his listeners take it too "literally," or, more likely, they don't take it seriously at all. That's just something they say in church! We have already mentioned that the main difficulty with that saying of Jesus is that we take the concepts of love and hate to be simply emotions (and not attitudes and conscious decisions, the *focus* of our life). Naturally we are well aware that "there is no accounting" for emotions and that feelings of resentment persist in spite of our good intentions to fulfill Jesus's outlandish command.

Here the pseudonymous author presents us with a new theological and spiritual stimulus to have the courage to accept those people whom we would normally not be inclined to—"the wicked and criminal." He doesn't tell us to love and accept their wickedness, or to ignore, downplay, or forgive their wicked deeds and characteristics. Nor does he urge us to have any emotional attachment toward them. He simply tells us that Christ is present in the humanity of *everybody* through the mystery of the Incarnation. He is "imprisoned" in the "wicked" because they have not allowed him his freedom, they have not allowed him to reign in their hearts and actions.

By realizing that they too "belong to Christ" (and hence to us too) we do not liberate those people from evil. So far we only liberate *our relationship to them*—by allowing Christ to enter our attitude to them as the faithful image of the Father, who "makes his sun rise on the evil and on the good, and sends rain on the righteous and on the unrighteous."[3] Just how much our attitude toward them and our way of thinking about them influences our behavior and actions, and how much our behavior can retroactively affect them, influence them and possibly change them, is another open chapter of this story.

Christ only ever comes as a challenge, a proposition, an invitation to follow him, an open possibility—as *The God Who May Be*. It is entirely foreign to him to pressure us to manipulate us or not respect our freedom. The God that Christ presents us with (through his words and his personality) addresses us and challenges us but never forces us to do anything. That is what our Christian witness should be like: we are here to broaden the horizon of "possible" (i.e., anticipated, usual, "logical," "natural" behavior—the way things are done, the way of the world) to include what to people who do not know God and don't take Christ seriously naturally seems impossible. This also—being here as an "alternative"—is part of our ministry of healing, liberation, and "driving out evil," of which many have a somewhat romantic perception.

The "supernatural" in day-to-day "exorcism" (driving out evil) does not consist of what gripping films about exorcists luridly describe. It is something quite different: the breaking down of the boundaries of "the possible," or what the world around us regards as "normal" and *natural*, by our "impossible" behavior. Yes, we are called on to perform miracles—if we understand miracles, not in a romantic or Enlightenment sense of "breaking natural laws," but as what they really are: *events that we have no right to expect in the given circumstances.*

The possible, as the philosopher Jacques Derrida declared (and it was repeated by many postmodern theologians for whom he has gradually become some kind of new "church father" of Christian postmodernity) is what lies within our capacities, or at least within the scope of our plans, desires, expectations, and imagination. The impossible is what totally breaks through this horizon and brings in something radically and divinely new—as art and religion do. That is why, in one of my earlier books, I called the Kingdom of God "the kingdom of the impossible" that is accessible only to "little faith," that is capable of "impossible things"—forgiving where one could revenge, giving where one could keep or even take, taking risks and sacrificing oneself for others where one could enjoy a quiet life and one's creature comforts.[4]

How many scars would be treated and how many injuries would never occur if we were capable of removing (at least in our imagination) the "enemy image" from many people (an image, moreover, that is often one that we project onto them)—and if we were capable of seeing Christ in them—without in any way having to idealize them? We will probably only manage it insofar as we are capable of acknowledging that Christ's image in us is also not entirely free of scratches, dust, or overpainting, and that it is not very easy for others to recognize!

The first step to healing the world's wounds is our conversion, repentance, humility—or in everyday language: the courage to be truthful about ourselves.

The church's confessionals are not—as people often imagine and as many desire and demand—washrooms where I can quickly and easily shower off what has soiled my ideal image of myself, where I can get rid of what disturbed my (false) peace of mind and go back to my pleasant illusions about my own innocence. Those who use and misuse the "sacrament of reconciliation" in this way (in the role of either confessor or the one confessing) more likely heap on themselves another truly grave sin (the grand lie, self-deception). Such people would scarcely understand the words (and life experience) of St. Augustine, who wrote that sins also (*etiam peccata*) can help us find the right path.[5]

They can help us when, at a moment of true repentance, "the scales fall from our eyes" and we discover truthfully our place and situation in the world—when we realize that in the age-old battle of good and evil, which fills the deep dimension of our history ("the history of salvation"), we are not and cannot be neutral observers, and certainly can't naively assume that our place is among "the good and the just." Our hearts are also in the front line of that battle, and our life is a battlefield on which we receive many wounds, which we must first expose if they are to be healed (and if they are to help us heal the wounds of others). They include also our painful traumas, both the forgotten and the never discovered, and those we don't admit to. They include disappointments and blows dealt by "fate," as well as wounds inflicted on us by others—and also the wounds that we have inflicted on others (maybe even in good faith), and which (even though we are often unaware of it) frequently damage us more than those wounds inflicted by others.

I say *mea culpa*—my fault—at the beginning of the mass, not so I will be hurled into the dust of hopeless self-recrimination and self-pity, but so I will come back to earth from the fake paradise of illusions about myself and experience God creating me anew (from the dust of the earth, *ex nihilo*—God's favorite material, after all!), and breathing his spirit into me.

Man is made of dust and the Spirit, the vivid image on the threshold of the Hebrew Bible tells us;[6] through sin, says the psalmist, people "return to their dust," but God forgives them and sends forth his Spirit, so that they are created again.[7]

We said that when Christ comes and shows us his wounds it can rouse our "courage for the truth," our courage to take off the "armor, masks, and makeup" that we use to conceal our wounds from others, and often from ourselves.

This concerns first and foremost our traumas, which are so present in us in spite of our efforts to forget them that they constantly draw our attention to them. People are often worn out by elaborate pretense or constant overexertion in an effort to conceal, overcome, or compensate for them. St. Ignatius's advice *agere contra* (to go against what our own inclination might be) is not appropriate in all cases; for instance, the constant joke telling of people suffering from depression can be somewhat tiring after a time. We really ought to face up to these traumas that demand our attention in this way and prevent our attempts at escape, compensation, or suppression. Often direct confrontation with these problems within ourselves is less tiring, painful, and dangerous than constantly fleeing from them.

When one is truly capable of relying on the assurance that God accepts us the way we are, including our traumas, sorrows, scars, and problems, then this awareness itself may sometimes offer an even safer place of rest (and respite from our own stress and demons) than a cushion on a psychoanalyst's couch. (This is not to say that I underestimate the assistance of a psychotherapist, which is necessary in many cases and should by no means be ruled out when seeking a spiritual route to inner reconciliation and healing.)

But of course there are traumas that we have "successfully" displaced or that never entered into the full light of our consciousness. If, either in prayer, on a psychoanalyst's couch, or at some other privileged moments of our life, these things return to our consciousness, then what applies are the words used by the Lord in so many Bible narratives when entering the world of humans: Be not afraid!

Yes, even something that emerges from the darkness of night and behaves for a long time as an enemy that we must do battle with, one that even wounds us, can eventually turn out to be a messenger from God. If we have fought it courageously it will bring us a blessing in the morning—remember the important scene in the Bible of Jacob's wrestling by the stream called Jabbok.[8]

The perfection that we are called on to seek in the Old and New Testaments is a matter not of flawlessness but of integrity, wholeness. The first step toward this integrity is the meekness that accompanies conversion: I'm *that* too!

What isn't accepted cannot be redeemed, the fathers of the church taught when contemplating the mystery of the Incarnation. The first thing that God wants of us when he grants us the grace to see our wounds (truly demanding grace, not cheap grace), *is to accept them* and be capable of saying "yes" even to these realities of our lives, even when we do not yet understand the reason for our "yes," even when we still harbor questions that are not yet fully answered: "Why?" and "Why me?"

It's all right for me to have wounds! This a hugely liberating step toward healing. I don't have to be strong and beautiful and successful like the heroes of movies and TV serials; I don't have to be glowingly happy, unassailably healthy, and eternally young like the shop-window dummies of ubiquitous commercials for everything and nothing; I don't need to have eyes blazing with determination, an extended hand, and a Colgate smile like the politicians on the (photoshopped) election posters.

God laughs at them[9]—just as he did when he came down to see the puny Babylonian skyscraper[10]—and we can laugh with him. It is very liberating to be allowed to be the way I really am.

At the moment of humble discovery (and acceptance) of what I really am, my authenticity, do I not become at last an authentic image once more of the one who is who he is? By accepting my imperfection do I not (paradoxically) take a decisive step in the direction of the integrity that he imprinted on man, as his seal, his image, but also as a mission and task?

The wounds I have been endowed with by "fate" and "others" I am allowed to have. To a certain extent they cease to be traumas if I accept them and if I endure my true nature, alleviated and liberated both from the burden of pretense and concealment and also from the dictate of advertising and external claims that force or tempt me to be what I'm not and what in reality I should not and cannot be.

But what about the wounds we have inflicted on others? And what about the wounds that are not just my private affair, because they have affected my circle of relationships? In this instance I cannot offer any surprisingly new recipes. Where I am able to apologize, I ought to apologize, where I can make amends I must make amends, where I ought to be reconciled, I must at least make an attempt.

Where I really cannot make up for what I have spoilt or neglected, I must be capable of letting go. In such cases it is important to have the courage to place such things into the flame of God's mercy, and, trusting in God's forgiveness, I must forgive myself. If my old faults have passed through the portal of prayer (or, in some cases, confession) to God, if I have submitted them to God's mercy, and if in conversation with God they have become *experience* for me (and prevent me from repeating them thoughtlessly), then it is an act of faith to release them forever. Then they can and should become for me what is finally past, a past that has been redeemed and submitted to God, a past that I must and should no longer concern myself with. And if feelings of guilt should still happen to flare up from that past, from the still too hot ashes of my memories, and no longer lead me toward healing humility but impede my capacity for joy, freedom, and doing good, then I must deal with them as I would any other temptation: chase it away like an annoying fly, ignore it as if it were a dog barking beyond the fence of a stranger's garden.

There are people who are incapable of believing in God's mercy, incapable of forgiving themselves, incapable of freeing themselves from feelings of guilt. They torment themselves with more and more acts of repentance, seeing sin everywhere, where there really is none. They are called scrupulants. Amedeo Cencini, an author of incisive analyses of frequent problems of spiritual life, regards scrupulants' behavior as an expression of narcissism:

So if a scrupulant accuses himself it is not delicacy of con-science, it is dictated by his ego (or super-ego) whose narcis-sism is offended, and it takes revenge and tries to re-stabilize itself, condemning itself and punishing itself in every possible manner. . . . This always contains an element of exhibitionism and a relentless yearning for utter perfection. . . . A scrupulant *never experiences forgiveness because he has never taken into account the real nature of his sin.* He lives in fear of discovering some real fault, and he doesn't admit that he really is a sinner; he sees sin in trivial matters in order to protect himself from the thought that he might have sinned in matters of importance.[11]

Scrupulants' constant doubts and self-torment stem from a narcis-sistic focus on their own ego, which is their *real* sin, and in the meantime they ignore God's love, and they will never know the lib-erating and healing truth that God's love *is greater than their sin.*[12]

We are summoned to live in the truth—the sin we are really to beware of is self-deception.

⌒ But isn't the separation of sins into sins "against oneself," "against others," and "against God," as we know them from tradi-tional "confession mirrors," and the similarly strict separation of injuries inflicted and suffered, actually an artificial division?

One is human insofar as one is human with others and for others. There are no "private sins" that concern me alone and do not affect others, and no actions of mine that harm others that do not at the same time harm myself. Even the deformation of myself in the most sealed chamber of my private life will eventually sap the power and authenticity of what I owe to others and what I ought to be for others and for the world. God—as our faith teaches us— created each of us as an irreplaceable original, and probably not at all out of the mere passion of a creator or collector of curios, but because—if I may be permitted to use naively anthropomorphic language (which the Bible itself does not shy away from)—God *needed* someone like that for his world, particularly for other people. If we fail to cherish and develop or actually spoil this original creation of God's and mar God's intention in making it, then we are not only harming ourselves but also cheating others, and are guilty of ingratitude and a failure to understand our Creator.

If we harm others, then, regardless of how much it might profit us in the competitive battles of our world, any such action (and, as Jesus taught, this also means word, attitude, and intent) is also inscribed in us. We too are part of that *creatio continua*—the eternal process of creation. For better or for worse we take part in God's unfinished creation of the world *and of ourselves*. We either creatively fulfill the intention of the creator or foolishly try to mar it. Our every day, our every act, word, and thought, leaves an impression on the vessel that we are on the Potter's ever-turning wheel.

Our humanity is constantly being formed not only by our common humanity but also by our fellowship with God and our relationship to God; at the same time our relationships to ourselves, to others, and to God are inseparably linked in manifold ways. One can also say: one is a human being insofar as one is a human with God, before God, and for God.

For God's sake, some will immediately object: you mean you don't consider atheists as fully human?

My response must be carefully differentiated. I am convinced that most people who declare themselves to be atheists are atheists "in name only"—they call themselves atheists because the mystery that is disclosed by Christian faith they do not call God. Nevertheless, it is obvious (and where it isn't we may assume) that they have an openness to that mystery, and sometimes it is profounder than in the case of many of us Christians. Our relationship to God the Father does not manifest itself by the way we call Him so, but by the way we behave toward our brothers and sisters. We demonstrate our relationship to God the Creator not just by our opinions about the creation of the world but more fundamentally by our relationship to nature. We demonstrate our relationship to the mystery of the Incarnation not only through the verse in the Creed that we recite with bowed head during a religious service but above all by what we do with our humanity and with the humanity of others.

Of course, apart from these atheists "in name only," who in many cases (and not only in those just mentioned) actually live the mystery of faith, there also exist genuine *existential atheists*, who demonstrate through their lack of respect for others, nature, and so on that they truly stand "on the other shore." And I'm sure I don't need to add that this kind of truly dangerous atheism (godlessness)—which is truly a human defect—is to be found not only among those who regard themselves as nonbelievers but also among those who regard themselves as pious believers.

No person has the right to determine who belongs to which category, for one thing because this dramatic contest between belief and nonbelief takes place in the heart of every human being if they are alive. It is up to Christ's Last Judgment to reveal to people whether they have ranged themselves on the "right side or the left" when the whole of their lives is taken into account—and it is clear from the gospel description of this scene that everyone is in for a surprise.[13]

Concerning repentance, we were speaking about the need to let go, to "surrender" certain facts that we cannot alter. Something similar applies to our relationship to other painful wounds that our hearts suffer in the form of great loss, particularly the loss of a dear one.

Of course, loss assumes a different form depending on whether a loved one has been taken by death or whether they have left us of their own accord. In the second case the pain of our grief is often intensified by a sense of being betrayed and deceived; we have to struggle not to allow our love to turn into hate, and instead of the remedy of forgiveness to reach for the poisonous drug of retribution. Nevertheless, every serious loss often involves a lengthy and painful process during which we generally go through phases that are well documented by psychologists: shock and reluctance to believe it; an attempt to "bargain" and an irrational longing to somehow "avert" or negate the painful event, followed by an inner struggle sometimes involving feeling of rage and revolt; and moments of resignation—before we finally achieve the peace of reconciliation—accepting the reality. (A number of authors mention that a similar process is undergone by people who learn that their illness is terminal and find themselves on the threshold of their own death, as well as by people who share the death of a loved one.)

At this time of trial and pain—particularly after we take final leave of someone who has died—the rituals of the church can contribute significantly to the healing of wounds, and likewise the rituals in the treasure chests of all the great religions (and sometimes ceremonies used by secular society in an attempt to copy and replace the ministry of the church). If we have been unable to heal all the wounds in our relations with our dear ones during their lives (and what close relationship does not bear any such scars?), it is still worth sending our inner forgiveness (and prayer for forgiveness) after them in the ceremony of farewell. Even when our notions of "life after death" may have paled into a vague question mark, if we take God at least a little bit seriously we do not abandon hope that the gate through which our departed have passed does not lead into "nothingness," and that even if they eventually fade from our memory God will be here forever as the depths of memory, in which everyone and everything remains preserved forever.

During the grieving process (*Trauerarbeit*, to borrow Freud's terminology), a period that it really doesn't pay to "skip," avoid, drown, or displace, we sometimes discover that after their life story has ended and they no longer live in front of us and with us, our loved ones "live in us" even more deeply and are more real—and we carry what they were for us a little further. But the time of mourning must also be a time and means for healing, not for reopening wounds. There comes a time we must really "let go" of our departed.

Here too faith plays a unique role: it gives us the courage and confidence to take this step, without having to worry that in doing so we are betraying or showing ingratitude to our departed. The gate that we let them pass through is not locked for good, and the barrier that separates us from them is not impenetrable. They are inaccessible only to our senses and to those people whose world ends at the limits of sensory cognition. But we have been entrusted with three paths that allow us (like the resurrected Jesus) to pass through even the locked gate of death to an inseparable fellowship. They are faith, hope and love, these three; and the one that most allows the dead to live is love.

If we really manage to accept our wounds—in the power of faith, in the confidence that God fully accepts us with them—they are thereby transformed. It doesn't mean they must necessarily stop hurting forever—even old scars and physical wounds sometimes make themselves felt in certain weathers—but they now occupy a completely different place in our lives, and our life itself is now fuller, more integrated, and more abundant.

There is an old Czech Easter hymn that speaks of the wounds of the resurrected Christ: *His wounds are healed and shine like precious stones*. And the great medieval German mystic St. Hildegard of Bingen taught that even our wounds *will change into pearls*.

Anselm Grün writes in this connection:

> The transformation of my own wounds into pearls means for me that I regard my wounds as something precious. Where I am wounded I am more sensitive toward other people. I understand them better. And where I am wounded I come into contact with my own heart, with my real being. I abandon the illusion of my strength, health, and perfection. I am aware of my own frailty, and this awareness makes me more real, more human, more merciful, and softer. My treasure is to be found in the place of my wound. There I come into contact with myself and my mission. I also uncover there my capacities. Only a wounded doctor knows how to heal.[14]

When he was acting as theological adviser to the Second Vatican Council, Karl Rahner, one of the greatest Catholic theologians of modern times, received a request from a Spanish priest that he should try to get the Council to give significant support to veneration of the Sacred Heart of Jesus. For several centuries during the late modern period this devotion—inspired by several female mystics—had become increasingly significant in popular religion, as well as in the liturgy of the church year and in official documents of the popes. The documents of the Second Vatican Council make absolutely no mention of it, however. In an essay inspired by that letter, Rahner wrote that maybe this type of devotion will become a relic of the past like the statue of the Infant of Prague in the dusty display cases of our grandmothers. It is one of the finest essays in the whole of Rahner's many-volumed oeuvre. Its title is "The Man with the Pierced Heart."[15]

Even if this devotion ceases to exist in popular religion, Rahner continues, maybe it will become the secret of the spirituality of the priest in times to come. What will the "priest of tomorrow" be like? He will be someone who involves himself in the hard lives of his brothers and sisters, someone who can be trusted and counted on. He won't be able to rely on the social power of the church but will have the courage to remain powerless. "Tomorrow's priest will be a man whose calling is most difficult of all to justify in profane terms, because his real success is always vanishing into the mystery of God and because he is not a psychotherapist dressed in the old-fashioned costume of a magician." He will give God the victory even if he succumbs in the process. He will see the effect of mercy where he could not provide the sacrament. His strength will not be measured by the statistics of confessions, and yet he will live in the conviction that he is God's servant and messenger, and this in spite of the fact that God's grace operates outside of him and without him. The priest of tomorrow, Rahner concludes, will be *a man with a pierced heart*, "pierced through by the godlessness of life, pierced through by the folly of love, pierced through by lack of success, pierced through by the experience of his own wretchedness and profound unreliability, believing that only such communicates the strength for his mission, that all the authority of office, all objective validity of the world, all the efficacy of the sacraments' opus operatum, are only turned into the event of salvation by the grace of God if they come to man through this ineffable channel of the pierced heart."

13

The Last Beatitude

Thomas believed in Christ because of what he saw. He saw wounds transformed into precious stones, he saw that pain was overcome and that suffering and death did not have the last word. So he could believe in what constitutes the core of Christian belief: a God who shows himself in Christ, in the Resurrection, in love that is stronger than death. But what about those who didn't see anything of the kind?

Thomas was followed by countless more people who did not have his healing experience, who did not see the sun rise after the night of pain, the sun whose wounds were still festering and painful. What can we offer *those who did not see*? They are the subject of Jesus's final Beatitude.

> *Blessed are the poor in spirit, for theirs is the kingdom*
> *of heaven.*
> *Blessed are those who mourn, for they will be comforted.*
> *Blessed are the meek, for they will inherit the earth.*
> *Blessed are those who hunger and thirst for righteousness,*
> *for they will be filled.*
> *Blessed are the merciful, for they will receive mercy.*
> *Blessed are the pure in heart, for they will see God.*
> *Blessed are the peacemakers, for they will be called children*
> *of God.*
> *Blessed are those who are persecuted for righteousness' sake,*
> *for theirs is the kingdom of heaven.*[1]

Who is not familiar with the eight Beatitudes, the ceremonial gateway to Jesus's Sermon on the Mount? At the end of John's

Gospel in the scene of his encounter with "doubting" Thomas, Jesus adds another, *final Beatitude*, when he says to the apostle: "Have you believed because you have seen me? *Blessed are those who have not seen and yet have come to believe.*"

Many gospel commentators maintain that the Beatitudes at the beginning of the Sermon on the Mount describe, not "eight types of people," but eight aspects of the same outlook on life of a disciple of Jesus. These are now joined by this ninth one.

Isn't this last Beatitude in fact a key to understanding the previous ones (or at least some of them)? Are we not poor, mourning and thirsting for righteousness *because*—or at least also because—we did not see and still cannot see? And even those who are pure in heart are so far only promised that *visio beatifica* (beatific vision); not even they "see" yet.

Jesus came into the world "so that those who do not see may see, and those who do see may become blind."[2] And when, after those words, the Pharisees, the smug "possessors of the truth," resentfully ask him, "Surely we are not blind, are we?" Jesus answers them, "If you were blind, you would not have sin. But now that you say, 'We see,' your sin remains."[3]

In the eight Beatitudes, Jesus prophetically turns our gaze from the past in which we did not see, and the present in which we still do not see, to the eschatological future of the Kingdom of God, where we will see God, where we will be filled, be comforted, and receive mercy . . . but he does not add any further promise to the last Beatitude. Does that mean those who endure the state of "not seeing" already have their reward in faith alone? Does it mean that faith alone fills this state with meaning, transforming it and conferring on it value and depth without removing the veil of mystery from sightless eyes? "Now faith is the assurance of things hoped for, the conviction of things not seen."[4]

In his encyclical *Spe salvi*, Pope Benedict recalls emphatically that the term *elenchos* (conviction) in that sentence means, not simply the subjective opinion of the believer, but a "proof" (*argumentum*):

Faith is not merely a personal reaching out towards things to come that are still totally absent: it gives us something. It gives us even now something of the reality we are waiting for, and this present reality constitutes for us a "proof" of the things that are still unseen. Faith draws the future into the present, so that it is no longer simply a "not yet." The fact that this future exists changes the present; the present is touched by the future reality, and thus the things of the future spill over into those of the present and those of the present into those of the future.

Faith is the substance (*hypostasis*) of what we hope for. That means, the pope says, that

> through faith, in a tentative way, or as we might say "in embryo"—and thus according to the "substance"—there are already present in us the things that are hoped for: the whole, true life. And precisely because the thing itself is already present, this presence of what is to come also creates certainty: this "thing" which must come is not yet visible in the external world (it does not "appear"), but because of the fact that, as an initial and dynamic reality, we carry it within us, a certain perception of it has even now come into existence.[5]

It is important that in this major commentary the pope places the words *proof* and *thing* in quotation marks. Proof in this context is not a proof as used in mathematics, or the natural sciences, or even philosophy or logic, which would not admit doubt and would definitively refute objections; the proof that we can and ought to provide "an unbelieving world" is our "witness," the testimony of our lives. The "thing" that faith relates to has not yet become a "deed," a fact that is evident to all—we can only enable a glimpse of it by our lives as witnesses. We have to "account for the hope" that is in us.[6]

But how are we to do so if we ourselves are among those "who have not seen"—and are even warned not to present ourselves as those who "see" and "know"? The answer is that we are asked to give an account, not of what we "see" or "think," or what our convictions are, but of our hopes, our faith, and our love. These are what we must prove and demonstrate, so that more light may penetrate the dark recesses of the world.

"Blessed are those who have not seen and *yet* have come to believe." Genuine faith, blessed faith, has always something of the "and yet" or "nevertheless" about it—of the courageous step of faith across the frontier of the verifiable and intelligible.

In the scene in which Jesus summons his first apostles and challenges them, after a night of futile efforts, to once more let down their nets, we already hear the first profession of faith by Peter, the future "priest of the apostles": we have caught nothing, *yet* if you say so, I will let down the nets![7]

Trust in his word yields hope. But for us now that word is for us the word of witnesses. The witnesses are to become that word, witnesses such as Thomas and also those that come after him, those who have not seen—and yet have come to believe. Insofar as our faith is capable of making this leap of trust and courage from "the seen world" that tempts us in many ways toward disbelief and mistrust, to the "unseen"—the embrace of the mystery of the hidden meaning of an incomprehensible and invisible "Reality"—we become "witnesses." Even our wounds, caused by painful encounters with the absurdities of the world, the wounds of unbelief and mistrust, which, if untreated and unhealed, could poison our hearts with despair, cynicism, and resignation, are now transformed.

And a transformed wound of unbelief is now to be the place where people who have not seen the Resurrected One and have not experienced power overcoming pain can touch and experience what Thomas did.

There is one important thing to add. That leap of faith, conversion (whether from a state of "unbelief" or one of formal, simply "inherited" belief), tends not to be a one-act drama. Faith in which there is always only the "beginning" and "germ" of what it relates to can never be permanently protected from subsequent repeated gusts of unbelief and doubt. After all, we encounter so many wounds in the world, which fill us again and again with painful questions about whether our trust in meaning is not just an illusory projection of our wishes. Sometimes the fascinating power of evil transfixes us and tries to suck all the courage and hope from us; at other times we are subject to the smug and ironic gaze of those who no longer expect anything because they "already have their reward" in what the world has to offer in terms of wealth, entertainment, and amusement, and where their treasure is, there is their heart also. The world and life are and always will be ambivalent, full of paradoxes, providing sufficient reasons for belief and unbelief depending on our own particular "setting." There is nothing *in them* that can definitively support our faith (which is something other than mere "conviction about the existence of God").

A living faith will be wounded over and over again and face crises. Yes, and sometimes it will be "destroyed." There are moments when our faith (or to put it less starkly, the existing form of our faith) wastes away—in order to be resurrected once more.

Yes, only a wounded faith with the visible "marks of the nails" is credible and capable of healing others. I fear that a faith that has not lived through a night of crisis and been "struck to the heart" does not have this power.

A faith that has never lost its sight, that has never experienced darkness, will scarcely help those who have not seen and do not see. The unwounded religion of the sinfully self-assured "sighted Pharisees" gives a stone in place of bread, ideology in place of faith, theory in place of witness, lecturing in place of help. And in place of the mercy of love it gives just prescriptions and proscriptions.

Not until the inability "to see" is honestly and humbly acknowledged can there be scope for faith. Faith is commanded to remain unseeing. It must strive to the very last to keep that space of "the unseen" *empty, but also open*—like the tabernacle on Easter Saturday when homage is paid to the wounds inflicted to Christ's body and heart. For that truly formidable challenge, faith also needs hope and love.

The jealousy of love does not allow the emptiness and purity of that space to be filled with any old "visions," illusions, or substitute gods. The patience of hope keeps that space *open*—so that those who enter it should be, not engulfed in the darkness of hopelessness, but already fortified by a ray from the place of light toward which faith is constantly heading but can never fully enter.

"If you manage to eat that whole portion on your own, you'll understand the language of birds," I say appreciatively, and with a serious face, to my little god-daughter Niké as she gazes with surprise at the huge plate of food just placed before her in a restaurant. "But I already understand them a bit," she laughs at me. "So what do they say," I inquire. "But it can't be translated into human speech, can it?" she says, shaking her head at my—typically adult—ignorance.

It's true—the speech of angels and birds cannot be fully translated into our speech however much we understand it, and it is the same with our body language. Touch has its own language that requires no words, as all tender lovers know. It is likewise known to wounded soldiers and people dying. And most sacraments are administered by touch.

"Who touched my clothes?" Jesus asks when surrounded by a crowd of bystanders. And the disciples are disrespectfully bewildered: "You see the crowd pressing in on you; how can you say, 'Who touched me?'" But no touch is anonymous to Jesus; he can easily make out the touch of yearning and trust of the woman suffering from hemorrhages.[8]

Nor can our theology do more than "touch the hem of his cloak," and it will be rid of its infirmities only when and if that touch is sufficiently respectful, while also full of longing and courage. To touch God—that's a contradiction in terms, isn't it? But the one who is the paradox of paradoxes through the mystery of the Incarnation permits and enables this touch—and particularly, as we said before, "in the dressing stations of the world," and not just in the dressing stations of the physically wounded. That is where we can touch him, where we can hold him in our hands, like the bread during the Eucharistic feast.

Our contact with Christ oscillates between "Don't touch me!" (his words to the Magdalene) and "Reach out your hand!" (his words to Thomas). It would be wrong to touch him if we sought to detain him on his way to the Father, if we wanted to *appropriate* him. We may and ought to touch him on his return on his "second coming," which already starts here and now in "the least" and culminates at the moment when his anonymous presence in "the least" becomes a record: "Just as you did it to one of the least of these who are members of my family, you did it to me."

I am now too old to understand the language of birds. I am still not simple and pure enough to understand the speech of the angels. But I can hear Christ speaking in the wounds of the world, I hear there his call and the beat of his heart: I can't fail to understand, I can't pretend deafness. And over and over again—and never sufficiently—I learn the language of touch that would answer his call, the art of touches that are gentle enough to bring relief to places of pain.

Written in the hermitage of a contemplative monastery in the Rhineland in July and August 2008, and completed on journeys to Jerusalem and Auschwitz in September of the same year.

NOTES

Chapter 1. The Gate of the Wounded

1. 1 Peter 3:15.

2. Friedrich Nietzsche, *The Gay Science: With a Prelude in Rhymes and an Appendix of Songs*, trans. Walter Kaufmann (New York: Vintage Books, 1974), 181.

3. Friedrich Nietzsche, *Thus Spoke Zarathustra: A Book for Everyone and No One* (New York: Penguin Classics, 1969), 201.

4. Cf. Romans 8:35.

5. Cf. John 20:20–27.

6. Cf. Matthew 12:33.

7. Cf. 1 John 4:1.

8. Cf. Matthew. 13:29.

9. Cf. Luke 18:25.

10. I wrote in greater detail about my Indian trip, including that day in Madras, in another of my books, *Co je bez chvění, není pevné* [What doesn't tremble isn't firm] (Prague: NLN, 2002), 25–28.

11. Cf. Matthew 7:21.

12. Cf. Matthew 4:3.

13. Cf. 1 John 4:20.

14. Cf. 1 Corinthians 1:17.

15. "Plus enim nobis Thomae infidelitas ad fidem quam fides credentium discipulorum profuit." *Hom.* 26.7–9 (PL 76:1201–2).

16. Cf. 1 Corinthians 13:4.

17. Cf. Song of Songs 8:6–7.

18. Cf. 1 John 4:16.

19. Cf. 1 Corinthians 4:10.

20. Exodus 3.

1. The story goes that once, when Pascal was refused the Eucharist by some church dignitary who had doubts about his orthodoxy, he started to care for some poor sick person in his home, so as to "receive the body of Christ" in that way. I ask myself to what extent even now something similar might be an inspiration for many who are prevented from approaching the altar for whatever reason (and maybe also for those of us who do approach the Eucharistic table).

2. Matthew 25:40.

3. Schelling seems to have felt something similar: "Thus in order that there be no evil, there would have to be no god himself." F. W. J. von Schelling, *Philosophical Investigations into the Essence of Human Freedom* (Albany: SUNY Press, 2007), 66.

4. As early as 534, Pope John II, when asked whether "Christ, our God, who, in his divinity is incapable of suffering, suffered in the flesh," sent the following unambiguous reply to Constantinople: "God truly suffered in the flesh."

5. John 1:1.

6. "Recognizing the beloved is god" is a quotation from Euripides's tragedy *Helen*. Kerényi adds: "The divine event was welcomed: Ecce Deus! Theos!, i.e. nominative, not vocative. . . . A divine event bursts in, *theos* happens, in time, in this world, and it happens entirely. If we eliminate the language barriers and with them the various semantic tricks the sentence will mean: God happens." Cf. Hans Waldenfels, *Kontextuelle Fundamentaltheologie* (Munich: Paderborn, 2000), 105.

7. 1 Timothy 2:5.

8. "At bottom there was only one Christian, and he died on the cross." Friedrich Nietzsche, *The Antichrist* (New York: Alfred A. Knopf, 1918), 112. Further, Jesus "denied that there was any gulf fixed between God and man; he *lived* this unity between God and man, and that was precisely *his* 'glad tidings'" (118); "The life eternal . . . is the life that lies in love free from all retreats and exclusions, from all keeping of distances" (93).

9. John 19:37 and Psalm 22:18 among others.

10. 1 Peter 2:24.

11. John 16:28.

12. Luke 22:53.

13. John 12:32.

14. Isaiah 53:2–3.

15. Psalm 22:6–7.

16. Lamentations 1:12.

17. John 18:38.

18. Friedrich Nietzsche, *Thus Spoke Zarathustra: A Book for Everyone and No One* (New York: Penguin Classics, 1969), 136.

19. John 18:36.

20. This interpretation of Jesus's sacrifice is dealt with most thoroughly in the works of René Girard, such as *The Scapegoat* (Baltimore: Johns Hopkins University Press, 1986).

21. Blaise Pascal, *Pensées*, no. 546, Gerald Turner's translation.

22. The phrase used is *"Shivim panim la'Torah"*—literally, "There are seventy faces to the Torah."

23. John 14:9.

24. Richard Kearney, *The God Who May Be: A Hermeneutics of Religion* (Bloomington: Indiana University Press, 2001).

25. Exodus 3.

26. Matthew 25:45.

27. John 14:6.

Chapter 3. *Arcanum Cordis*

1. Bernard of Clairvaux, *Canticum Sermones*, sermo 61 (PL 183:1072).

2. Luke 23:28.

3. Cf. Colossians 1:24.

4. "Nonindifférence" is also a favorite concept of Emmanuel Lévinas.

5. Mark 15:34.

6. The impact of those words cannot be lessened even by reference to the fact that it is a quotation from Psalm 22, which has an "optimistic" ending.

7. Cf. Galatians 3:13, Romans 8:3.

8. G. K. Chesterton, *Orthodoxy* (San Francisco: Ignatius Press, 1995), 145.

Chapter 4. A Torn Veil

1. Cf. Matthew 27:51 and Hebrews 10:19–20.

2. According to patristic commentaries, just as Eve was born out of the side of Adam, so also the "eternal woman" of the church was born out

of Christ's opened side. (Similarly, Mary, standing beneath the cross, and in some representations holding "the holy grail," a chalice catching the blood from the heart, is seen as a symbol of the church, which is both Mother and Bride—through its preaching and sacraments, the church ceaselessly "gives birth to Christ" in the souls of people and nations.)

3. Philippians 2:7.

4. Hebrews 10:20.

5. Ephesians 2:14.

6. Miroslav Volf, *Exclusion and Embrace* (Nashville, TN: Abingdon Press, 1996), 126.

7. The Jewish theologian, journalist, and historian of Christianity Schalom Ben-Chorin maintained that the exclusiveness of the covenant (restricted solely to the Jews) is characteristic chiefly of pre-exile Judaism, whereas in the Babylonian exile, and subsequently in the diaspora, the idea of universality started to emerge; this would inspire and be radically developed by Paul, as a Jew of the diaspora; see Schalom Ben-Chorim, *Paulus: Der Völkerapostel in jüdischer Sicht* (Munich: List, 1970), 170–79. According to other authors, however, "universalism" was present in Judaism from the very outset: *erev rav*—a multitude of non-Jews—joined the Israelites on their departure from Egypt; during Succoth sacrifice was made for other nations; Jonah spoke of the conversion of the pagan seamen; etc.

8. Christianity as the fulfillment, examination, surmounting, and termination of the sacrificial mechanism is a major theme in the religionist works of René Girard; see chiefly *The Scapegoat* (Baltimore: Johns Hopkins University Press, 1986). In fact, however, sacrificial offerings came to an end in Judaism with the fall of the Temple in the year 70. The rabbinical authorities transferred the symbolism of the sacrifice from "blood sacrifices" to "lip sacrifice," i.e., praise.

9. Cf. Hebrews 7–10, particularly 10:18–22.

10. Cf. Hans Urs von Balthasar, *Mysterium paschale*, in vol. 3, pt. 2 of *Mysterium salutis*, ed. Johannes Feiner and Magnus Löhrer (Einsiedeln: Benziger, ca. 1965–ca. 1976), 214.

11. 2 Corinthians 3:14–15.

12. "Wenn ich heute dieses Bildnis der Synagoge mit den verbundenen Augen anschaue, dann bewegt und beunruhigt mich die Frage, was diese Augen wohl gesehen haben." J. B. Metz, *Memoria passionis* (Freiburg: Herder, 2006), 63–64.

13. Metz repeatedly attributes the authorship of this expression to Nelly Sachs, without citing an actual source (see ibid., 8, 68, and 101).

Nelly Sachs, "Landscape of Screams," *Poems of Nelly Sachs in English* (blog), April 28, 2013, translated by Catherine Sommer, https://nellysachs english.wordpress.com/2013/04/28/landscape-of-screams/.

14. The idea of divine self-contraction (*tsimtsum*) originates in the Lurian Kabbalah, named after Isaac Luria (1534–72).

15. Hans Jonas, *Der Gottesbegriff nach Auschwitz* (Frankfurt: Suhrkamp, 1984).

16. Ekkehard Schuster, Johann Baptist Metz, Elie Wiesel, and Reinhold Boschert-Kimmig, *Hope against Hope: Johann Baptist Metz and Elie Wiesel Speak Out on the Holocaust* (New York: Paulist Press, 1999), 91.

17. Robert McAfee-Brown, *Elie Wiesel: Messenger to All Humanity*, rev. ed. (Notre Dame, IN: University of Notre Dame Press, 1994).

18. My translation from Martin Luther, *Luther Deutsch: Die Werke in neuer Auswahl für die Gegenwart*, ed. K. Aland (Stuttgart: Klotz, 1960–69), 1:162.

19. My translation from Gerhard Ebeling, *Dogmatik des Christlichen Glaubens* (Tübingen: J. C. B. Mohr, 1979), 1:256.

20. Regarding the remarkable similarity between the biographies, character, and theological and spiritual themes of Luther and Teresa of Avila, see, for example, Waltraud Herbstrith, ed., *Teresa von Avila, Martin Luther: Grosse Gestalten kirchlicher Reform* (Munich: Kaffke, 1983).

21. Of course, a number of themes of the "death of God theology" are being developed in a new context by postmodern theology that is close to my own thinking and draws on elements of "apophatic theology" in late Derrida. These include the provocative and inspirational attempt by Gianni Vattimo to perceive secular society as the "age of the Holy Spirit," and "weak" metaphysical thought as an analogy of the kenosis of the Son of God on the cross. See Gianni Vattimo, *After Christianity* (New York: Columbia University Press, 2002), 20.

22. It should be added that in the light of the latest research Hochhuth's play looks more like an instrument of the antichurch propaganda of the GDR at that time—in reality Pope Pius XII was not as passive in the face of the Jews' suffering as that play and similar publications described.

23. Philippians 3:8; 1 Corinthians 2:2.

24. I have in mind, for instance, Thomas Altizer's contention, mentioned earlier, that there was a God, but since the death of Jesus that God is dead. God is now identical with humanity or the history of humanity.

25. Cf. John 14:18.

26. Similarly, but in another context, Herbert Braun writes: "Atheist verfehlt den Menschen" (*Gesammelte Studien zum Neuen Testament und seiner Umwelt* [Tubingen: Mohr, 1971], 341).

27. Cf. Jung's letter to Pastor Fritz Pfafflin in *Letters of C. G. Jung*, vol. 1, *1906–1950*, ed. Gerhard Adler and Aniela Jaffé (London: Routledge, 2015), 191–92.

28. Jan Patočka, *Heretical Essays in the Philosophy of History*, trans. Erazim V. Kohák (Chicago: Open Court, 1996), 108, emphasis added.

Chapter 5. A Dancing God

1. Richard Kearney, "The God Who May Be—Part 2," conversation with David Caley, CBC radio, January 15, 2007, www.cbc.ca/player /play/1473883496, 46:00.

2. Friedrich Nietzsche, *Thus Spoke Zarathustra: A Book for Everyone and No One* (New York: Penguin Classics, 1969), 68.

3. Cf. Mark 10:15; John 3:7.

4. Cf. Nietzsche, *Thus Spake Zarathustra*, 54.

5. My translation of Tomasz Weclawski, *Królowanie Boga: Dwa objaśnienia wyznania wiary Kościoła* (Poznań: Uniwersytet im. Adama Mickiewicza, 2003), 139.

6. Ibid., 230–31.

7. Romans 6:9.

8. Galatians 2:20.

9. Cf. Romans 8:9.

10. According to Feuerbach's theory of God as a projection of human "essence" onto heaven, man empties himself, whereas in denying God, he "breathes" again and recaptures the greatness taken from him. We tend to adhere to Paul's theory of the cross as kenosis—in the sacrifice of his Son, God is "emptied." According to the Gospels Jesus on the cross expired—gave up the Spirit (*tradidit Spiritum*)—so that in that same Spirit we may attain the glory, greatness, and freedom of God's children.

11. John 14:28.

12. John 4:24.

13. John 16:7.

14. Dietrich Bonhoeffer, *Letters and Papers from Prison*, ed. Eberhard Bethge (New York: Touchstone, 1997), 359.

1. Stanley Hauervas, Richard Bondi, and David B. Burrell, *Truthfulness and Tragedy: Further Investigations in Christian Ethics* (Notre Dame: University of Notre Dame Press, 1997).

2. In this part of my reflections—assessing the "war on terrorism" and its corollary—I indirectly quote and only slightly develop the critical reflections and observations of Richard Kearney in "The God Who May Be—Part 3," his conversation with David Caley, CBC radio, January 22, 2007.

3. Ibid. Here Kearney refers to his own analyses in his book *Strangers, Gods and Monsters: Interpreting Otherness* (London: Routledge, 2003).

4. Contemporary exegesis interprets the words "I am who I am" not as God's providing a name or as a metaphysical definition (the one whose essence and existence are one, whose being is also his essence) but rather as God's *refusal* to grant Moses's wish to be told the name of God.

5. Cf. John 14:13.

6. For an excellent introduction to this form of prayer, which is the most practical and profound I have ever known, see Moine de l'Eglise d'Orient, *On the Invocation of the Name of Jesus* (San Bernardino, CA: Borgo Press, 1986), Wilfrid Stinissen, *Deep Calls to Deep: A Study in Christian Depth-Meditation* (Basingstoke: Marshall Pickering, 1988), and particularly Franz Jalics, *Contemplative Retreat* (Munich: Xulon Press, 2003).

7. John 14:26.

8. *The Sacred Writings of Clement of Alexandria*, ed. Philip Schaff (Altenmünster: Jazzybee, 2017), 1:57.

9. Cf. Galatians 6:14.

10. Galatians 5:24.

11. Miroslav Volf, *Exclusion and Embrace* (Nashville, TN: Abingdon Press, 1996) 24.

12. Revelation 5:8–9.

Chapter 7.   Stigmata and Forgiveness

1. John 20:19–23.

2. E.g., Mark 12:1–8.

3. Cf. Matthew 21:41.

4. René Girard, in particular, paid great attention in his works to this aspect of Easter, for example in *The Scapegoat* (Baltimore: Johns Hopkins University Press, 1986). The paschal drama is also dealt with in the spirit of Girard by the theologian Raymund Schwager in *Jesus in the Drama of Salvation: Toward a Biblical Doctrine of Redemption*, trans. James G. Williams and Paul Haddon (New York: Crossroad, 1999).

Chapter 8. Knocking on the Wall

1. Simone Weil, *Gravity and Grace* (London: Routledge, 2002).

2. Zuzana Svobodová, *Nelhostejnost: Črty k (ne)náboženské výchově* (Prague: Malvern, 2005).

3. Cf. Acts 1:11.

4. "Ich beschwöre euch, meine Brüder, bleibt der Erde treu und glaubt denen nicht, welche euch von überirdischen Hoffnungen reden! Giftmischer sind es, ob sie es wissen oder nicht." Friedrich Nietzsche, Zarathustras Vorrede § 3, in *Also sprach Zarathustra: Ein Büch für Alle und Keinen* (Leipzig: C. G. Naumann, 1907), 9.

5. Cf. Exodus 3:5.

6. See Matthew 13:44.

7. Matthew 13:38.

8. Cf. Romans 2:28–29.

9. Cf. Matthew 6:25 and 33.

10. Cf. Elias Vella, *Ježíš—lékař těla i duše* (Kostelní Vydří: Karmelitánské nakladatelství, 2006).

11. Friedrich Nietzsche, *Thus Spake Zarathustra*, I. The Three Metamorphoses (Project Gutenberg, 1999), http://eremita.di.uminho.pt/guten berg/1/9/9/1998/1998-h/1998-h.htm#link2H_4 _0006.

Chapter 9. Bodies

1. A sign was posted outside the synagogue saying "If you enter with your head uncovered, it's as if you've committed adultery!" The next day someone wrote underneath: "I tried both, but there's no comparison!"

2. More about this (and about "icon theology") in chapter 11.

1. Cf. John 17:14–19.

2. But not even here do we "see" God. God is here more like the light in which we see the world, people, and ourselves.

3. Miroslav Volf, *Exclusion and Embrace* (Nashville, TN: Abingdon Press, 1996), 271.

4. My translation of Martin Luther, *Luther Deutsch: Die Werke in neuer Auswahl für die Gegenwart*, ed. K. Aland (Stuttgart: Klotz, 1960–69), 1:146 et seq.

5. 2 Corinthians 7:5.

6. I am deeply concerned to witness the occasional problematic use and misuse of the term *charism of truth* in our Catholic Church as a synonym for *charism of office*. If some church dignitary interprets and uses it in a naive and arrogant sense, reminiscent more of the thinking of communist functionaries, i.e., "If I have an official function, then anything I say must be taken as the truth," it not only is a theological and moral error (the dogma of papal infallibility and doctrine on the role of the magisterium in the church cannot be vulgarized and arbitrarily "extended" in this way) but also can be a grave sin against the spirit of the gospel. ("Coming to terms with the communist past," which the church often calls for, should also comprise vigilance with respect to this unconscious and unacknowledged legacy of totalitarianism.)

7. Volf, *Exclusion and Embrace*, 272–73.

1. According to hints in the Gospels and particularly the apocryphal scriptures, Mary Magdalene truly had a very close human relationship with Jesus. Attempts to make much more of those apocryphal allusions by present-day writers, verging on sensationalism and pulp fiction, are probably worthy of careful theological and psychoanalytic study. It strikes me that fantasizing about Jesus's marriage and parenthood betrays something similar to the media's fascination with the topic of celibacy and the sexual problems and misdemeanors of the clergy (although I don't mean to make light of those issues in the least): Jesus's celibacy and priestly celibacy, like everything that might call into doubt the sacralization and

absolutization of sexuality in an age when sexuality has become a major commodity in a society of consumerism and entertainment, must be discredited and stamped out!

2. Cf. John 20:1, 11–18.

3. Fundamentalism is a typical heresy of modern times; it consists of naively substituting a "literal" i.e., superficial, reading of the text that is burdened with every modern prejudice as the only true "original meaning." Fundamentalism invokes tradition but it is radically antitraditional. It disregards the fact that in the dramatic flow of tradition, the constant transmission of a text from generation to generation, there have been so many "paradigm shifts" in the understanding of the meaning of words, etc., that there is a need for theological hermeneutics—the search for the original context, and regard for the genre of the text, for its "Sitz im Leben." The church, theologians, and indeed the New Testament itself (cf. 2 Peter 1:20) always emphatically warned against the hasty and naive "private interpretations" that the fundamentalists indulge in.

4. Cf. Matthew 17:4.

5. Cf. Genesis 1:31.

6. Let us repeat: current exegesis stresses that the "I am who I am" (or, more precisely, "I will be the one who I will be") is not a "name" but rather a refusal to reveal "a name" such as people use to invoke their gods (and by no means is it a metaphysical definition of the essence of God, even though that idea has borne rich philosophical fruit in history).

7. Cf. Exodus 33:23.

8. Cf. Matthew 7:21.

9. John 14:12.

10. Cf. Matthew 5:1–10.

11. Cf. 2 Corinthians 3:12–18.

12. Genesis 1:2.

13. Luke 1:35.

14. Cf. John 15:26—the expression *Parakleitos* can be translated as "Comforter" or "Advocate."

Chapter 12.   Wounds Transformed

1. Luke 24:39.

2. Moine de l'Eglise d'Orient, *On the Invocation of the Name of Jesus* (San Bernardino, CA: Borgo Press, 1986).

3. Cf. Matthew 5:45.

4. Tomáš Halík, *Night of the Confessor: Christian Faith in an Age of Uncertainty* (New York: Crown, 2012).

5. Augustine was commenting on St. Paul's words "We know that all things work together for good for those who love God, who are called according to his purpose" (Romans 8:28)—*etiam peccata*, and also sins! It would also seem to be the intention of the deliberately provocative sentence (which has naturally scandalized many) by the erstwhile Augustinian monk Martin Luther: "Sin boldly!" Awareness of sin can open up those who show regret, repentance, and humility to the gift of God's grace; those who consider themselves righteous never open themselves to this gift because of their proud, closed nature.

6. Cf. Genesis 2:7.

7. Cf. Psalm 104:29–30.

8. Cf. Genesis 32:23–33.

9. Psalm 2:4.

10. Genesis 11:5.

11. Amedeo Cencini, *To Live Reconciled* (Bombay: St. Paul Publications, 1988).

12. Cf. 1 John 3:19–20.

13. Matthew 25:31–46.

14. My translation of Anselm Grün, "Duchovní cesta jako cesta uzdravení," in *Máš před sebou všechny mé cesty: Sborník k 60. narozeninám Tomáše Halíka*, ed. Zdeňka Nováková (Prague: Nakladatelství Lidové noviny, 2008), 107–8.

15. Karl Rahner, "The Man with the Pierced Heart," in *Servants of the Lord* (London: Burns and Oates, 1968), 107–19.

Chapter 13.   The Last Beatitude

1. Matthew 5:1–10.

2. John 9:39.

3. John 9:40–41.

4. Hebrews 11:1.

5. Pope Benedict XVI's encyclical *Saved in Hope* (*Spe Salvi*), 2007, chap. 7.

6. Cf. 1 Peter 3:15.

7. Cf. Luke 5:5.

8. Cf. Mark 5:25–34. For more about this pericope, see Tomáš Halík, *Patience with God: The Story of Zacchaeus Continuing in Us* (New York: Doubleday, 2009), 171–75.

TOMÁŠ HALÍK is a Czech Roman Catholic priest, philosopher, theologian, and scholar. He is a professor of sociology at Charles University in Prague, pastor of the Academic Parish of St. Salvator Church in Prague, president of the Czech Christian Academy, and a winner of the Templeton Prize. His previous books with University of Notre Dame Press, *I Want You to Be* (2016, 2019) and *From the Underground Church to Freedom* (2019), were selected as the Foreword Reviews' INDIES Book of the Year Awards in Philosophy and in Religion, respectively.

GERALD TURNER has translated numerous authors from Czechoslovakia, including Václav Havel, Ivan Klíma, and Ludvík Vaculík, among others. He received the US PEN Translation Award in 2004.